HYENAS IN MY BEDROOM

Hyenas in My Bedroom

By Jack Mohr

SOUTH BRUNSWICK
NEW YORK: A. S. BARNES AND COMPANY
LONDON: THOMAS YOSELOFF LTD

Library of Congress Catalogue Card Number: 68-12251

A.S. Barnes and Co., Inc.

Cranbury, New Jersey 08512

Thomas Yoseloff Ltd
108 New Bond St.
London W. 1, England

SBN
498-06673-8

Printed in the United States of America

Acknowledgments

This book is dedicated to Aud and Bosse Grythe of Oslo, Norway, who spent fourteen years in Ethiopia and who were instrumental in getting me started on it. I also want to remember Cookie, Fadul, Mohammed, Abraham, and my crazy American compatriots. Most of all, it is dedicated to the American taxpayer, who paid the tab which resulted in fifty-four months of unusual adventure. All incidents recorded are true as are names of the characters mentioned.

Contents

List of Illustrations

Introduction

Sitting behind the dubious protection of a thorny African hunting blind, I could feel the short hairs on the back of my neck stand on end. For hours Pat and I had been sitting there like a couple of Oriental idols. We couldn't afford to move, not even to swat at the pesky mosquitoes which seemed to find every crevice in our head nets. A sharp thorn had been working its insidious way into my rump for the better part of an hour, but every time I tried to shift, it brought a low, but profane, reprimand from my companion.

Now after this long wait, something sinister was moving around just outside the shoulder-high enclosure we had so carefully made from the branches of an acacia thorn bush. It wasn't the leopard we had been waiting for the past two nights, of that we were sure. This thing sent out definite signals of danger which seemed to react on our sixth sense like beams on a radar. There was an aura of evil out there that awakened feelings which had lain dormant for centuries; possibly the same feelings experienced by some distant ancestor when a saber-tooth tiger roamed just outside the circle of his fire.

9

When a person becomes frightened, either by the known or the unknown, every sound and movement is magnified into something which becomes at once huge and terrifying. I thought back to the numberless nights in Korea, when I had sat frozen in a cramped outpost, scarcely daring to breathe, while I listened to the scrape of branches and strained my eyes for a foreign movement in the stygian darkness. This was the same way I felt tonight. My nerves were drawn tight to the point of screaming. To add to the illusion, an illusive, disagreeable odor drifted in to us on the faint night breeze.

Straining my eyes until they ached, I tried to pierce the darkness which lay outside like some dark velvet blanket. All I could see were imaginary shapes which kept changing before my tired eyes. As I took a stronger grip on the stock of my double barrel 12 gauge shotgun, I noticed for the first time that my hands were sweating. A good sign of fear is sweat that turns to clamminess on one's brow.

It was a cool night on that African river bank. The heat of the fierce noonday sun had been dissipated by a cooling breeze which blew in from the river. The sand under us was still warm, but I knew that before long, the night air would take on a frosty coolness. Now, every fiber of my being was tuned in on that evil presence outside. There was nothing to see in the absolute darkness except myriads of brilliant stars overhead. There was nothing to hear but the occasional snap of a twig, the snuffling of something evil and the pad, pad, pad of big feet on the sand outside.

The odor came again, washing in on a stronger breeze, until my stomach almost turned over in revolt. It was an odor combining the worst qualities of death and decay—a smell which might have come from a freshly opened grave. There was no question in my mind, I was frightened; but my pride kept me from calling out to the man who sat motionless a few feet away.

Suddenly, from close at hand, so close that it seemed to be almost inside the enclosure with us, came a wavering, whooping, maniacal scream, which died away in a series of insane chuckles. It was a sound such as might have been made by some mythical, demented woman crying over her lost lover. There was a moment of shocked silence. I felt like screaming too, for that cry took me back to my childhood, to a day when my collie had been crushed by a passing truck.

For the first time, the silence inside the blind was broken. My companion laughed.

"Scary isn't it?" he said. "The first time I heard one of those fellows, I thought for sure I was a gonner."

"What in heavens name is it?" I asked.

"Nothing to worry about, you know. It's only old "fisi," a spotted hyena to you novices. You couldn't get that old boy in here with us if you tried."

"My gosh, who'd want him in here the way he smells," I quipped.

Pat shined his powerful flashlight out towards the water hole. The brilliant beam of light revealed one of the most repugnant, yet amusing looking creatures I had ever seen. If you have ever seen a hyena in a zoo, let me assure you they look much different when on the loose only a few feet away. Looking at the old boy, I wanted to laugh, but I couldn't—a sort of creepy aftermath to the scare he had given me. When the odd-looking animal found that he had been discovered, he wrinkled his awful face in a sneer, gave another of his spine-tingling cries and ambled off into the darkness.

"I wonder if that spotted devil will show up tonite?" Pat

queried, "or are we just sitting here wasting our time and losing some sleep? We'll wait a couple more hours until midnight and if he doesn't show up, we'll call it a day. I'll bet that old bastard is sitting off in the brush somewhere laughing at us now."

We had been sitting in this same blind for two nights, waiting for a big leopard to come to the putrid bait of warthog carcass which was rotting in the river bed fifty yards away. For two nights we had strained our eyes and ears, watching for the big devil. He had outsmarted us every time. Each morning, we would find fresh, pug marks made when he crept up close to where we were waiting. We knew he was a big cat, for the marks made by his feet were huge. On the second night, he had been within ten feet of our blind. I was beginning to believe some of the stories I had heard about the devilish cunning of the big, spotted cats. They are rated among the most dangerous animals in Africa, even though they are smaller than some of the other animals that roam the veldt country.

The night began to quiet down again and the usual sounds drifted in to our ears: The constant stridulating of the cicadas, as they tuned up for their part in the great African symphony. The distant, sleepy cursing of a herd of baboon came from near the river . . . possibly they had been disturbed by a hunting leopard; maybe the very one we were waiting for. Farther up the stream, the darkness was shattered from time to time by the booming, deep-mouthed roar of a lion, as he sought to make the night miserable for a herd of Thompson gazelles. The cry of the hunter and the screams of the hunted, blended into a cacophony of sound.

The darkness of an African night is total. There is nothing I know of that compares with this intense pitch darkness;

it is a blackout of light which is so thick it can actually be felt, like some hot, oppressive blanket. The night had come upon us within a few moments, like the dropping of a huge, black velvet stage curtain. One minute the sun glowed fiery red on the western horizon, painting the cumulus clouds overhead a vivid scarlet; the next instant it was dark. This is a strange phenomena which takes place in many places in the tropics.

As I leaned back against the wheel of the Land Rover, around which we had built our hunting blind and let the smoke from my cigar trickle from my lips, I let my mind drift back over the incidents which had landed me in Africa.

It's not every boy who can realize his childhood dreams and one day find himself viewing strange sights he has only read about before.

The story of how a Michigan farm boy ended up on the veldt of Africa is too long and boring to tell here, except for a few details which are necessary in explanation.

I was a Sergeant First Class in the United States Army, assigned to Kagnew Station. This is an outpost of the Army Security Agency, located in the city of Asmara, Eritrea the capital of the northernmost province of Ethiopia.

In 1957, after having served fifteen years in the army, and having worked my way up through the ranks from a private to the rank of lieutenant colonel, I came to a decision which was to have a decided effect on my life. I was serving an assignment in Lincoln, Nebraska, at this time, as an advisor to the Army Reserve Units of Southeast Nebraska. The blow fell in the summer of 1957.

With a huge cut-back in the armed forces, I was one of some 5,000 reserve officers who were given the choice of getting out of the service or reverting back to my permanent enlisted grade. It came as rather a shock to me, for I had been promoted only a few months before and my record had been excellent, except for a few times when I had tangled with senior officers. With fifteen years of service behind me, I could not afford to quit. In August 1957, I gave up the silver oak leaves of a lieuteant colonel and donned the five stripes of a SFC.

The change from officer status to that of enlisted man meant going through considerable red tape. During this process, I was offered a job with the Army Security Agency, destination Ethiopia. I jumped at this opportunity, for I loved to travel and I had never been to this part of the world. My hour of trial had somehow turned into an unseen blessing, for I was to see with my own eyes the country I had dreamed of for so many years and old "Uncle Sam" was going to pay the bill.

I reached back to scratch the spot where a persistent ant had worked his way up my pant leg and was industriously trying to make off with part of my leg. The warmth of the sand made me sleepy. It was a subtle reminder of the 120 degree heat that had scorched these same sands at high noon. I knew that in a little while, the warmth of a jacket would feel good and by morning we would welcome the protection of a wool sleeping bag. It was not unusual to wake in the morning out here on the veldt to find the ground covered with hoar frost.

There was a slight sound outside the blind, almost like the movement of air against your skin. As Pat turned on the powerful spotlight, we saw outlined in the blinding circle of light two beautiful hunting cheetahs. They stared at the light for a moment, then in one powerful, graceful leap were out of sight. They moved so quickly, it seemed possible they had not been there in the first place.

"Beautiful creatures, aren't they," he said. "They are said

to be the fastest of all four-footed beasts. Some say they can travel over seventy miles per hour for a short distance. I have an Italian friend in Asmara, a doctor, who keeps one for a pet; darndest thing you ever saw. That big cat follows him around like a dog. They are protected here. I've seen as many as thirty in one night, as they come to a waterhole.

We sat back to enjoy another smoke. We knew for sure that old leopard wasn't coming tonight. Pat continued:

"They look a lot like a leopard, but are a bit smaller and not at all vicious. Maybe you noticed their heads looked more like a dog, than a cat. Their feet are the same too. If you were to examine them, you would find they can't retract their claws like a cat. Some day if you are lucky, you may see one of them run down a gazelle. There is nothing in the animal kingdom which matches them for sheer speed and breathtaking gracefulness."

As the cigar smoke drifted up on the vagrant breeze, my thoughts drifted back once again to the months just passed. In February 1958, I climbed aboard a Super Constellation of the Military Air Transport System at McCord Airforce Base in New Jersey on the first leg of the trip to Africa. Our destination was Orly Field in Paris. In the French capital, we boarded a TWA DC-6 which took us over the Alps to Athens. There we boarded a two-engined Convair, painted vivid green, yellow and red—the colors of Ethiopian Airlines. The Lion of the Tribe of Judah was rampant on it's side.

Within moments after leaving the ground at Athens, we were winging our way south across the Mediterranean Sea. With a full moon overhead, the silver paths over the calm sea far below were fantastic to see. After a brief refueling stop in Cairo, where we were kept inside the terminal by zealous Egyptian army guards, we headed south again across the deltas of the Nile River and the desert, for another stop at Port Sudan on the Red Sea.

A new adventure lay just ahead. As our plane flew low over the jumbled rocks and endless sands of the desert, it was easy to imagine the passage of some caravan—loaded with spices, precious metals, and very probably contraband, or even slaves for some harem in Saudi Arabia. Without closing my eyes, I could visualise the chariots of Pharaoh, as he pursued the Jews towards the Red Sea, almost thirty-five centuries before.

In a little while, the sands of the desert gave way to rugged mountains and our plane began to rise. Asmara, perched like an eagle's nest on the top of a 7,800-foot mountain plateau, is one of the few airfields in the world where a pilot must gain altitude in order to land.

Althought Asmara is in Ethiopia, it is essentially an Italian city. Built to be the capital city of Mussolini's East African Empire, it still retains much of the grandeur it must have possessed in the thirties. Now the European population has dwindled from over 100,000 to less than 15,000. Today the city reflects it's Italian heritage, as much of the main part of the city is strictly Italian in architectural design.

The Eritrean landscape is wildly rugged and beautiful. It seems almost impossible that such rugged and forbidding country can still thrill a person with it's wild beauty. Huge rocks have been tossed about the mountain sides in jagged profusion, as though they had been playthings of some facetious giant. In between and round about grow cactus, thorn bushes, and the pale green eucalyptus trees. It is a forbidding, yet primitively beautiful country.

Most of the people of Ethiopia are dark skinned, yet they are extremely sensitive about being called Negro. For the most part, they are tall, handsome people, with high cheek bones, thin lips, high-bridged noses, and the slightly slanted eyes, which can be seen in paintings of ancient Egyptians. They are proud folks, for until the Italians overran their country in the 1930's, using modern planes and poison gas, they had been unconquered for over 1800 years.

I was brought back to reality by the annoying buzz of a persistent mosquito who had found his way inside my headnet. In spite of the advertised merits of *Off*, he was trying to get a sample of my blood.

"Someday I'm going to write a book about this country," I promised myself. "It's going to be about the people and the wonderful animals which inhabit this area. It will be written strictly for those who will get a vicarious pleasure from visiting Africa through the pages of a book."

This is the book I promised to write. There is no pretense at a plot. There is no continuity to its chapers. It is a collection of stories about hunting, animals, and people who fascinated me and who I hope will interest you. It is my wish that you may get many hours of delightful reading as we tour East Africa together, and that for a little while I may be able to take your mind off the cares of this bustling old world of ours.

This story concerns an amateur; one who tries to learn the ropes of a dangerous and always interesting trade. It is about a man who has no teacher and who learns mostly through being a student in the University of Hard Knocks. It is the story of a beginner, who gets into all sorts of amusing and sometimes dangerous predicaments.

All the incidents mentioned in this book are true. As in most hunting stories, some levity has been used to make the reading a bit more interesting. If you should happen to be in this book, I'm sure you will recognize yourself.

Special thanks go to Bert Klineburgher, president of Jonas

Brothers of Seattle, for the information he so generously gave regarding safaris to East Africa.

Thanks are not enough for Norma Clement, the lovely wife of my pastor, Rev. John Clement. Norma has been an enormous help to me in proofreading this book and in suggestions she made which will make it more readable. It goes without saying that I appreciate John's consideration in allowing her to help; his moral support went a long way towards success of this book, especially when I became discouraged. If this book is a success, they are both due a trip to Africa, where they can check for themselves on some of the stories which seemed to them to be a bit farfetched.

HYENAS IN MY BEDROOM

1 The Story of a Queen

My primary interest in Africa was the wild animals, but the hunting season was still two months away; so I decided to learn as much as possible about this fascinating country, it's people and customs. At the first opportunity, I drove south to the ancient capital city of Axsum. At one time, centuries ago, this little village of straw and mud huts was the largest and richest city in Africa, boasting a population of over a million and a half people. Today, it is surrounded by the crumbling remnants of a once mighty civilization. This was the capital of the Queen of Sheba's fabulous empire, which matched in grandeur the civilizations of the Egyptian pharaohs farther to the north.

Axsum is an eight-hour drive south from Asmara. The first fifty miles are over one of the few paved roads in Eritrea. The rest of the way you take potluck, as your car bounces over the dusty, washboard roads which make up most of the first-class highways in Ethiopia.

It is an interesting trip. Starting from Asmara, perched on the top of a 7800-foot mountain, you follow the plateau for a number of miles, until suddenly, without warning,

21

the road drops over the rim of cliffs which make up the northern edge of the Great Rift Valley. This valley extends hundreds of miles south into Kenya. About fifty miles north of Axsum is the city of Aduwa, which figures prominently in the modern history of Ethiopia. It was here in 1896 that the savage tribesmen of Emperor Menelek II, armed primarily with swords, spears, and bows, defeated the modern army of King Victor Emmanuel of Italy. The invading force was almost annihilated in this humiliating defeat, which was avenged years later by the legions of Mussolini.

The old capital of Ethiopia sits in the center of a vast plateau, which is now under intense cultivation. As you enter the city from the north, the only sign of modern civilization is a lovely little hostelry run by a German lady. Here you can savor the modern conveniences while you rub elbows with an ancient civilization which is less than five minutes walk away.

No one knows the exact age of this old civilization. Historians disagree, but most believe it to be over 5,000 years old. History shows that it was at the height of its glory in 1000 B.C.

On the south side of the present village stands the oldest Coptic church in Ethiopia. This is the state church with the emperor as its titular head. The old building made of stone, held together with mortar-like mud, has been standing for some 850 years. If your stomach is strong enough to stand the stench, or if you are not afraid to walk barefooted among the many lepers with their suppurating sores, you may enter the sanctuary. There are two primary rules in evidence here—no women and no shoes. The women worship at a smaller church located some distance away.

The history of the Coptic church is depicted in vivid and often gory fashion on the fading murals which decorate the walls and ceiling of this stone building. Starting with the conversion of the Ethiopian eunuch by the Apostle Philip about 37 A.D., as told in Acts 8:27 of the New Testament, the history of this unique church is told in picture form down through the last of the Coptic saints. Their patron saint seems to be Saint George. The story they tell of his fight with the dragon is similar to that told farther north. I was amused to see that the good saint was depicted with a black face, as he killed an Ethiopian type dragon. The Virgin Mary and Christ himself were depicted with dark skin.

Mixed with the religious murals are others, telling in detail the story of the fabulous Queen of Sheba and her relationship with the Hebrew King Solomon.

If you are fortunate enough to find the priest in charge in an amicable mood, a mood which can be greatly enhanced by a generous contribution of money, he will show you the crown jewels of Ethiopia which are said to date back to the Queen of Sheba and are worth a king's ransom.

Ancient historians said that Ethiopia was the cradle of many of the religious cults which abound in the Middle East today, including the ancient religions of Egypt and Sudan. It came as no surprise to me to find that the Coptic religion had been infiltrated by many of the ancient customs of other religions, plus a generous dabbling in the art of the native witch doctors.

This area is also responsible for some of the most marvelous arts and sciences which came from the ancient world and which are lost today, or which cannot be duplicated. Traces of this ancient greatness can be seen in the ruins of Axsum. Here, carved out of the solid rock of mountains, or laying under towering obelisks, may be seen tombs of the old kings.

Possibly the most fascinating mystery of this city is the giant obelisk, a towering monument which engineers estimate may weigh as much as 1700 tons. It is carved from a solid piece of rock, a type which does not exist within 800 miles of this area. Some experts think this huge piece of stone may have come from across the Red Sea, from the vicinity of Yemen. How this huge stone was moved up the almost sheer cliffs of the plateau and across rugged desert and mountain trails is a mystery which baffles modern archeologists. I talked with one American engineer who had seen this huge monument. He was quite frank in stating that there is no modern machinery in the world today which is capable of transporting and erecting this monument. Somewhere in the dim past of civilizations which are now lying in the dust, there were engineers who held this secret.

Another mystery is the inscription on its base, which has never been deciphered. The towering stone, standing among the ruins of lesser monuments, is believed to be over 5,000 years old.

Wandering down the narrow cobblestone streets of this ancient city, I could almost hear the whisper of past glories. It was not necessary to close my eyes, to see in my mind the passing parades of queens and emperors. I thrilled to think of the intrigue that must have been present here in this greatest city on the continent of mystery.

An old beggar, crying the mournful call of the beggar clan, "Baksheeshi, baksheeshi, baksheeshi!" drew my attention. I stopped to drop a few coins in the cup held in his outstretched claw of a hand. As the coins tinkled into the metal cup, I was startled as he thanked me in almost perfect English.

For the first time, I really looked at the old man. He was

a man of imposing appearance in spite of the decrepit condition of his clothes which seemed to have been thrown on his gaunt frame. His eyes, dark as a mid-summer storm, peered out from under beetling brows that only partially concealed their fierce glare. They were emphasized by the deep bags underneath. Both eyes had been inflamed from exposure to the rays of the tropical sun, until yellow matter trickled in their corners. A scar, white against the duskiness of his face, ran a jagged course from the corner of his thin lips to his left ear. His mouth was made up of tightly compressed lips, which were partially hid beneath a scraggly, tobacco-stained moustache. His hair was dirty gray and fell in long, tangled locks to his stooped shoulders. Most of his face was concealed beneath an equally dirty beard that stretched from ear to ear. His face was set in a constantly sad expression, as though mirroring the melancholy of his innermost thoughts. His body was tall and thin, almost to the point of emaciation. The thing that really set him apart from the other natives was his voice—a deep, drum-like bass which must have been quite terrifying when he was angry. His whole appearance reminded me of the pictures of patriarchs I had seen in my Bible Story book as a boy. Dressed in once white robes and leaning on a long gnarled staff, he made a perfect patriarch.

In conversation with this remarkable man, I discovered he had spent several years in England, where he studied at Oxford University. I asked why a man of his background should be begging and he looked at me with obvious surprise and answered:

"But I am a priest and this is what the priests must do."

He agreed to show me the city for a small fee.

"I will tell you things you have never heard about the ancient glories of Abyssinia," he said. "Few people know, but this country rivalled anything the Egyptian pharaohs produced in the Nile Deltas."

We walked together to his home, up a winding cobble stone path, to a typical mud, stone, and straw hut. There sitting on a straw mat that had been tossed on the dirt floor and already feeling the invasion of a horde of hungry fleas, I sat entranced as he told me something of the fascinating history of his country. An incongruous note was injected into the scene by the graduate sheepskin from the famous English university, that reposed serenely on the fly-specked wall.

"It all started," he said in his deep voice, "with the loveliest princess Abyssinia had ever known."

"In the dim ages of Ethiopia's history, more than 1,000 years before the time of Christ, this princess had adorned herself with gold and jewels and, with a mighty retinue, had made the long, dangerous journey to Jerusalem to meet a king who was as handsome and famous as herself. Merchants coming into her kingdom from Palestine had entered that part of her country now known as Yemen. They came with great caravans loaded with gold. Their mission to obtain costly building stones, which their King Solomon wanted for the building of a temple in Jerusalem, which was to honor his God, Yahweh.

These merchants said that their king was not only very handsome and extremely wealthy, but that he was known far and wide for his great wisdom. His mouth was fairly overflowing with stories, they said; especially stories of love. There were some who disagreed as to whether he knew more about wisdom, or women. Who can say where one ends and the other begins.

As the queen journeyed to visit Solomon, she brought with her a wonderful array of gifts. These gifts are recorded in part in the 9th chapter of II Chronicles, in the Holy Scriptures: "And she gave the king 120 talents of gold (about $3,153,600 in our money) and of spices and precious stones great abundance . . ."

The old man hesitated in his story to refresh himself from a stone flagon of homemade beer which sat at his elbow. He wiped off the foam on the hem of his garment. Obviously he had used this same robe for a napkin many times in the past, for it was stained with many things. Then he continued:

"The day of the queen's departure from Jerusalem drew near and her caravan was laden with gifts from the Jewish ruler. For some time, the queen had been aware of a growing restlessness in the king. For all his wisdom, he was still very foolish where a beautiful woman was concerned. So she relaxed her decorum a bit, arguing with herself, no doubt, as women sometimes do, that she would be leaving the next day anyhow. She told the delighted king that she would spend the last night of her stay in his palace, if he would swear not to molest her. In return, she promised not to lay hands on anything that belonged to him.

"The king in his wisdom was said to have grasped the double meaning in her words. Just to make sure, he ordered his chief cook to prepare a marvelous meal and to season it with special care. There were delicacies such as tongues of peacock, breasts of guinea, and hearts of humming birds. Of course there was plenty of the heady wine for which the kingdom of Solomon was noted. When the queen saw that her host understood her and when she was alone with him, no doubt helped out by liberal draughts of wine, she had only to say, 'I will release you from your vow, o king, if only you will give me some fresh, cool water to drink.' The courteous Jewish king fulfilled her desires in every way and the day of her departure was postponed indefinitely. There is much more to this story, my friend," said the patriarch, "but I am an old man and very tired. I must rest. Come back tomorrow with a little more money and I will tell you much more."

That night at the little inn, I had a wonderful dinner of sauerbratten and then spent a comfortable but restless night trying to get some sleep. No matter how comfortable your bed, it's not easy to sleep when several hyenas are wandering around outside your bedroom window, conversing in the peculiarly insane way that only hyenas have. It was not until months later and after having heard them talk on many a night, that I was able to sleep through their diabolical serenades.

I didn't mind too much, for my mind was filled with delicious visions of a lovely dusky queen and a handsome king. The words from Solomon's Song rang in my mind, long after the electric generator died and the last light flickered out. "I am black, but comely, o daughters of Jerusalem, as the tents of Kedar, as the curtains of Solomon . . . behold thou art fair my love, behold thou art fair . . . there is no spot in thee . . . how much better is thy love than wine . . . "

Early the next morning I was at the hut of my English speaking friend. His name was Gebreghesier. The sight of a few Ethiopian dollars, worth 40c American each, was all that was necessary to get him started on his story.

"Going back to our story of the queen," he said, "months have now passed since the feast in the king's palace. The queen's condition was becoming very obvious to everyone in court. She decided to depart so that the child might be born in Ethiopia. With Solomon's songs to wing her on her way, she started for home."

Here he stopped the story and with a faraway look in

his deep set eyes, he began to chant in his deep voice:

"Who is she that looketh forth as the morning, fair as the moon, clear as the sun . . . return, return, o Shu' lamite; return, return, that we may look upon thee."

He sighed deeply: "Truly our queen must have been of great beauty." He continued: "On the way back to Axsum, the queen gave birth to a son and named him Menelek ibn Hakim, which means literally the 'son of wisdom.'"

"About twenty years later," he said, after refreshing himself from the beer flagon, "Menelek I, now the first emperor of Ethiopia, visited his father in Jerusalem. Solomon received him with great rejoicing. After a long stay, his father sped him on his way with many lavish gifts, including some of the jewels which may still be seen among the crown jewels. He was accompanied by Jewish priests, who were to instruct the Ethiopians in the Jewish religion.

"Menelek had scarcely left Jerusalem when the king's household and the temple were thrown into an uproar. The high priest discovered that the tables of stone, on which Moses had written the Ten Commandments of Yahweh, were missing from the Ark of the Covenant. Later Menelek was to say that the Jewish priests accompanying him had stolen them without his knowledge. Solomon swore the priests to secrecy and set off in pursuit of the robbers, but they had disappeared into the fastnesses of the desert."

The old man chuckled as he continued: "When Solomon found the tablets were gone for good, he had a good forger make another set and these were placed in the Ark. Even to this day, the Jews think they have the true tablets of Moses, but they are really here in Ethiopia."

I asked him where they were kept and he shrugged his shoulders: "I do not know," he said. "They are hidden somewhere." He stopped for a moment and peered at me

from under his beetling brows, then he said that the joke
Menelek had pulled on the very wise Solomon was one of
the classic jokes of the ages. "But then," he said, with a
twinkle in his eyes, "we Ethiopians have fooled many wise
people down through the years."

He told of other legends woven around the queen. One
was that she had prophesized the death of Christ on the
cross over a thousand years before it had happened.

"If you do not believe this," he said, "look on the walls of
any Coptic church and you will find this scene has been
depicted for hundreds of years."

"In this way a dynasty was founded which was to last in
historic times from 100 B.C. to about 800 A.D." With great
pride the old man said, "It lasted longer in the Mediterranean area than any other civilization."

He went on to talk about Ethiopia down through the
ages. "Is it any wonder to you, my friend, that a modern
ruler of Ethiopia, when he sought to establish himself as
emperor, proclaimed that he was a direct descendant of the
royal house of Solomon and took the title of Menelek II?
Today you can see his image on Ethiopian coins."

"The province of Eritrea, where you live," he said, "is
divided population wise, about equally between the Copts
who live in the highlands and the Moslem dogs who predom-
inate in the hot, dusty lowlands. Because of this almost equal
division between two religions which are diametrically op-
posed, the history this country has been a stormy one, with
many chapters written in blood and torture. Even today, this
enmity lies close to the surface."

"In 730 B.C. the Ethiopians invaded and conquered much
of lower Sudan and Egypt and brought back many of the
Egyptian gods and customs. Some of these religious customs
intermingled later with our Coptic faith.

"From this city of Axsum, the rulers of ancient Ethiopia ruled a vast empire that rivalled anything seen in the ancient world. It included all of present Ethiopia, plus most of what is now modern Egypt, Sudan, and Saudi Arabia. Later under Christian rulers, the Ethiopians became the bitter enemies of the Moslems and at one time, we lay siege to the Moslem holy city of Mecca." (This was in 622 A.D. the year the prophet Mohammed was born)

Later while studying further into the history of this fascinating country, I found that much of it's history was indeed strange and terrible. When the Copts were not fighting the Moslems, they were engaged in a fanatical fight against the inroads of the Roman Catholic Church. During these periods, rulers and priest alike turned their followers loose and people were hacked to pieces in the streets and fed to the wild dogs.

Bidding my priestly friend farewell the next day, I headed farther south, over the 11,000-foot mountain pass which guards the approach to the Middle Ages city of Gondar. Located in the high mountains just north of Lake Tana, which is the second largest fresh water lake in Africa, it is built on the same architectural lines as the Portuguese fortress city of Toledo.

In 1541, the king of Portugal heard about a Christian nation in the highlands of Africa, which was engaged in a heroic fight against overwhelming hordes of Saracens. With visions of the crusades still in men's minds, he sent a relief expedition around the Horn, under the command of the son of the famous explorer Vasca da Gama. From his base camp in what is now Kenya, da Gama marched overland from Mombasa on the Indian Ocean. Today, the frowning rock fortress of De Jesus still stands in Mombasa, as a monument to this gallant band.

After a march of 1500 miles across a dangerous and savage land, they were annihilated by a Moslem attack that used the human wave tactics now employed by the Communist Chinese. Within two years, another Portuguese expedition met the Mohammedans and decisively defeated them. They exacted revenge, literally, member for member.

During the fifteenth century, sectarian disputes about Christianity waxed furiously between various sects in Ethiopia, much as they were doing between Protestant and Catholic in Europe. Priests of these sects set loose their rabid followers with sword, spear, and fire, to slaughter, rape, burn, and pillage their brethren, over interpretation of the same doctrines which were causing slaughter among their so called civilized brothers farther to the north.

The first organized attempt to invade Ethiopia in modern times came in the late 1800's, when King Victor Emmanuel of Italy invaded Ethiopia through the province of Eritrea in the north. Using the seaport city of Massawa on the Red Sea as a base, the Italians strengthened their army with native volunteers and headed inland across the desert. They were not equipped to cope with the deadly heat which often reaches 150 degrees in the summer and many died from sunstroke and heat exhaustion. They finally fought their way into the mountain fastness of Asmara and from there made their way south towards the capital city of Addis Ababa.

In 1896, at the city of Aduwa, the modern, well-equipped forces of the Italian Army were met by the spear-wielding forces of Emperor Menelek II and soundly defeated.

Emperor Menelek II died in 1913 in his seventieth year, a victim of poison administered by his fifth wife. Before he died, he had united his country, after a period of anarchy which had lasted for a century and a half; he had made one nation out of seven kingdoms and several territories.

Today, after many years of rule by its modern and enlightened ruler Emperor Haile Selassie, this nation still retains areas of basic savagery. One such area is found near Lake Tana, close to the border of Sudan. Here a savage tribe lives which demands that before a man marries, he must bring to his intended the sex organs of an enemy; these she dries and hangs around her neck as a potency charm. To a man deeply in love, anyone becomes his enemy and it is needless to say there are few tourists in this area.

This was the country in which I was to spend over four years of my life. I was determined that most of this time, if possible, would not be spent in the cities, but in the fascinating and sometimes dangerous areas of the hinterland.

2 Hunting Family Style

One of the first peculiarities I noticed about the Americans stationed in Eritrea was that the conversation of both male and female centered on the subject of hunting. I have been a hunting enthusiast and conservationist for years, but nowhere have I found such enthusiastic nimrods as here. Wherever one went, whether in the NCO Club, the Mess Hall, in the barracks, or in private homes, invariably before the evening was over the subject would turn to hunting.

"What is the best way to hunt leopard? Can you kill a lion safely with a .30-.06 rifle? Is the cape buffalo as dangerous and hard to kill as they say? Are the wart hog and baboon dangerous? Will the hyena ever attack a human?" These questions were always answered by some personal experience, which was used to prove a point. The arguments would go on into the small hours of the morning, with the women more than holding their own.

It was quite obvious to me, within a short time, that the most vociferous were the rank amateurs who had possibly been on one safari and who were now trying to impress their listeners with their great fund of knowledge. This is not unusual, for hunters and fishermen are a breed apart and are quite peculiar when compared with normal members of the human race. Most of us are plagued with a burning desire to appear as experts in the eyes of our friends.

I decided almost at once that I wanted to become a real expert; one who could talk with authority about the country and its animals. I began to spend more and more time with the real pro's, men who had been out on safari many times and who knew what they were talking about. I found that to be a good listener was a real art. It was hard for me to keep quiet when men were talking about a subject of such interest to me; more so in that I am not known for my reticence.

Many of the real pros could back up their stories with pictures taken in the field, or, better yet, point with pride at some trophy hanging on the wall and say, "I got him on the Baraka River."

There were some who came to Eritrea and purchased mounted heads from local taxidermists. The experts looked on these men with obvious disgust, for they were frauds. Many homes looked like miniature museums and I often wondered at the wonderful spirit shown by the wives, who allowed these dust catchers to clutter up the walls of their homes. I put it down to the fact that nearly everyone, male and female, young and old, had been bitten by the "hunting bug."

Homes which would normally have had a few pictures hanging on the walls, now sported heads of gazelle, baboon, the snarling mask of a hyena, or the grotesque face of that ugliest of all animals the wart hog. In some cases the hunter could point with pride at the head of a great spiraled horned antelope, the greater or major kudu. (Sportsmen from all over the world spend thousands of dollars for one of these rare animals, which is high on the list of major game trophies.)

A few homes boasted divan covers made from the lovely pelts of leopard, zebra, colobus monkey, or lion. Sometimes the "little lady" would point with pride at one of these trophies and say, "That one is mine. I got him with one shot from my Winchester .270, at 386 paces, using a 150-grain boat-tail bullet."

One of the men to whom I was deeply indebted for my early hunting education was an American sergeant of Italian descent, by the name of Dominic Scalici. Dom was on his third tour of duty in Eritrea. He was not only a good hunter, he was also a sportsman. His home was decorated with trophies of twenty-seven different types of game he had shot himself. They ranged from tiny, graceful dik-dik, the smallest of the gazelle family, to a huge cape buffalo which took up the entire wall of one room and glared out from under a boss that centered horns 48 inches in length.

For many years I had been an avid hunter. I did not shoot for the fun of killing. Once I had a good trophy, I received more satisfaction from taking pictures of wild animals. The thrill of the stalk is still there. In fact it takes more skill to become a good wild animal photographer than a hunter and it is considerably more dangerous where big game is concerned.

This was a new type of hunting to me and I had to unlearn many things I had used while hunting in the States. Here was a country in which the animal you were stalking could and often would fight back, and where the hunter could very well become the hunted. As the hunting season approached, the tension grew until it seemed as though I couldn't wait for that first day to arrive. I was thrilled when one of the old timers asked me to go along on the first trip of the season.

This first trip was to be a short one, into the Mansura area, which is noted for the size of its wart hogs and for the large herds of unusually fine gazelle that graze there. Nowhere in the world have I ever seen such bird hunting; it is literally a shotgunners paradise. The area abounds with huge flocks of guinea fowl, francolina, and sand grouse. It was convenient to Kagnew Station, for it could be reached in an eight-hour drive and three of these hours were on paved roads.

The hunting permits had already been purchased at the cost of $5 U.S. They were good for five gazelle, seven wild pigs, and any amount of baboon, hyena, and fowl. Some of the rarer animals such as leopard, kudu, ibex, roan antelope, Sommering gazelle, and cheetah could only be taken with special permits. These were difficult to obtain, as they had to be signed by the chief executive.

For my first trip, I carried a Savage Model 99F, lever-action rifle, in .308 caliber, mounted with a 2x by 9x variable scope. In addition there was a Browning .22 automatic rifle, a Marlin .12 gauge super-posed shotgun, and a .45 caliber Colt Automatic pistol.

The commanding officer of Kagnew Station was an avid hunter. He made arrangements for the service men to be supplied with government transportation for their hunting trips. Gasoline was furnished by the hunters, who also paid a small maintenance fee for the use of the vehicles.

Army Special Services section had a limited amount of equipment available on a first come, first served basis. For the men who owned no weapons of their own, there were shotguns and rifles. There was a good supply of folding cots, blankets, gasoline lanterns, cooking sets, mosquito nets, gasoline and water cans, trailers, and huge ice chests which would hold up to 500 pounds of ice and which would last a large party for a five-day trip. They also had several jeeps and two Dodge Power Wagon, 3/4 ton trucks. These could be rented for the nominal sum of $2 per vehicle per day.

Our first hunt was to be a family affair and I was invited to take my eight-year-old son Dwight along. Unfortunately, my wife disliked the out-of-doors and was strictly a city-type gal. This was to be Dwight's first hunting trip and he was excited of course. The other members of our party were Master Sergeant Pat Gilbert, his petite wife Janie, and their fourteen-year-old son Rocky. Then there was the family of Master Sergeant Eddie Engleman, with his lovely blonde wife Ellie and their beautiful seven-year-old daughter Debbie.

We were to travel in two jeeps, both privately owned and both pulling trailers. I was to drive one of the Dodge trucks, pulling a trailer with a big ice chest.

The day finally arrived. Sleep came slowly to me that night and I was awake and up by three in the morning. Soon I heard the patter of bare feet and Dwight came into the kitchen, sleepy eyed yet eager to go. From the bedroom came a sleepy call: "What are you fools up to at this ungodly hour?"

Early morning in Asmara is cold in the spring of the year. The 7800-foot altitude calls for woolen shirts and warm jackets. As the truck I was to drive had an open cab, it was undeniably coolish, but nothing could cool my enthusiasm this morning. Everything was beautiful, starting with the delicious aroma of freshly brewed coffee and the smell of bacon frying.

I was interested to note that on the front pumper of each vehicle was a little plate bearing the likeness of an American flag. Pat flew a larger one on the hood of his vehicle. Some people thought that "shiftas," armed hill bandits, would not fire on American vehicles marked with a flag.

Dwight voted to ride with Debbie in the lead jeep, so

that left me with the native help, Cookie our camp boy, and Fadul the cook. Fadul was a Sudanese Moslem who worked for the NCO Club. By special arrangements, he was allowed to accompany members during the hunting season. He was a short, fat, roly-poly character, who always sported a big grin on his coal black face. He never went without his turban and prayer rug.

Fadul was a man of vast talent when it came to field cooking. In spite of the fact he was Moslem and detested pigs, he could cook wild pork until it literally "melted in your mouth." His accomplishments with a few victuals cooked over an open fire were truly amazing.

The vehicles were loaded until the springs groaned in protest. We were seldom able to exceed 40 mph on the twisting mountain roads. I was glad for this leisurely pace, as it was my first trip into this part of the country.

It was May, the middle of the dry season. Most of the country was barren except for the eternal green of the eucalyptus trees and the huge cactus which seem to stand guard over most of the Eritrean landscape.

The paved road wound north from Asmara along the top of the plateau for about ten miles. There was little to see of interest here, except for native villagers with their herds of cattle and donkeys.

Eritean roads seem to be always covered with people and animals during daylight hours. Most of the people are on foot, with a few mounted on donkeys and an occasional Ras (chief) riding by on a fine Arabian horse. The few busses seen are decrepit affairs, jammed to overflowing with humanity, goats, chickens, and sometimes a pig. The people hang from the doors and windows, while some perch on the roof, looking for all the world like outlandish white vultures, their white robes flapping in the wind.

It is hazardous driving in Eritrea, for no one supervises

the herds of animals which wander along the side of the highway. When there is a keeper, they pay very little attention to the animals in their care. At night, one must be on a constant outlook for donkeys which love to lie on the macadam surface that retains the heat of the day.

On hilly sections of road, there are always large boulders lying in the center of the highway. Most of these have been used to block the wheels or trucks or busses, which seem to stop in the middle of the road for no reason whatsoever and then drive on, leaving the rocks for the next motorist to hit.

Cattle slow travel more than anything else, as they move in a slow, resistless tide down the narrow roads in herds often numbering into the hundreds. Neither horn blowing nor shouts will hurry them up. They were large, vicious animals, with horns like the old-time Texas longhorn and with more than a strain of Brahma showing in their blood. The best way to get these bovine roadblocks moving was to ease your vehicle into the mass of animals and slowly push them out of the way. One day this almost backfired for me, when a large, irate bull, resentful of being butted in the rear, whirled on the jeep and proceeded to demolish its radiator.

This first day, the cattle didn't bother me. I was in Africa, on my first hunting trip. Everything was new and exciting and I loved every moment of it.

About thirty minutes north of Asmara, the scenery begins to change abruptly, as the road rounds a steep curve and proceeds to run along the side of a rugged mountain. A magnificent valley lies several thousand feet below and to the left, with a little ribbon of a stream meandering peacefully at the bottom. Across the valley, some twenty or more miles away, are the rugged peaks of the mountains which ring the Mansura plains on three sides. It seemed as though you could reach out and touch them. Everything was magnified in the clear air. We still had over a hundred miles to travel before we would enter the valley they formed. Our trip would take us in a half circle around them and we would enter from the northwest.

With little warning other than a road sign which said: "Change to second gear," written in English and Italian, the road began an abrupt descent of some 3,000 feet, following one breathtaking hairpin curve after another. As we reached the lower level, the frosty air of the mountain top gave place to a warm, gentle breeze which barely stirred the dry grass beside the road. The countryside took on a new charm and beauty. Cactus plants dotted the hillsides, while there were many trees which resembled the Joshua trees of our southwest plains. These stood with spiked arms akimbo, like stark sentries.

For the first time, we began to see signs of animal life. A covey of francolina, that quail-like bird, which is blessed with having only delicious white meat, scurried across the highway ahead of us. Occasionally, as the morning sunlight began to warm the mountain sides, we could see the slinking forms of jackals, as they returned to their dens from a night's hunting expedition. Once on a hilltop across the valley, we saw a herd of baboons, led by a grizzled old male. They stopped to curse us in their shrill voices, the first of many times I was to receive their sardonic insults.

A little farther down the road, two sau-sau played a game of follow the leader, as they leaped nimble-footed from one rock to another. These funny looking little animals belong to the gazelle family. We have nothing that approximates them in the western hemisphere. They do not possess the graceful bodies of the rest of the gazelle clan, but are fat as butterballs, with stiff, bristly, gray hair. In size they may reach the weight of a small policedog. The males have short spike horns. Although you may not be impressed with his graceful appearance, he is the champion jumper of Africa. I saw one make a standing leap straight into the air, to land on a narrow ledge at least ten feet overhead. The early Dutch settlers in South Africa called these little fellows "Klipspringers," which literally means "cliff jumper."

Sau-sau are found all over East Africa from the Cape of Good Hope to northern Ethiopia. They are alert little creatures which utter a shrill whistle when their curiosity is aroused. In some places they are called "African Chamois." When frightened, they will fairly bounce up the face of an almost perpendicular cliff like a rubber ball, finding footing on rocky projections the size of a quarter. The horns of the male are ringed at the base and rise almost straight up from their head. They make excellent pets and are very playful. Dom Scalici had one which loved to walk its sure-footed way along the top of a single layer brick wall all of ten foot high. It would leap on and off this wall, from the ground, with apparently little or no effort.

Soon the road dropped again, a few hundred feet this time, into one of the loveliest valleys in all Eritrea. As far as the eye can see, this valley is covered with a fruit plantation. Orderly rows of lime, lemon, orange, papaya, and mango trees march away towards the distant mountains, while the roadside hedges are covered with honeysuckle, bouginvillaea and frangipani. A small stream meanders through the valley to empty into a large lake at the north end. This lake, formed by a large earthen dam, holds the water used to irrigate the plantation.

Farther north, the fruit trees give way to huge fields of tomatoes. A large, modern bottling factory sits close to the highway, surrounded by the neat, white homes of the plantation workers. These homes are equipped with glass windows and screens, electricity and running water; items of rarity even in the larger cities. Nearby is a modern school, a hospital, store, and a large Roman Catholic Church.

The man responsible for this unusual complex was an ex-Italian nobleman. In the turbulent thirties, he was exiled from Rome because of his opposition to Mussolini's program of dictatorship. With the end of World War II, Emperor Haile Selassie returned to power and this foreigner became a citizen of Eritrea. For his good will towards the Ethiopian people, the emperor granted the use of his land tax free. Most of the money he saves by this arrangement goes back into improvement of the plantation and the working and living conditions of his laborers. He was one of the few foreigners I met in Ethiopia who is truly loved by the native people.

After leaving this modern Utopia, the road climbs a few hundred feet, to pass a police station built on a rocky promontory like some castle from the Middle Ages. Block-houses rise at each corner of a stone wall surrounding the central building. This is one of the many police strongholds found in the outcountry; designed to be used as strongpoints against robbers that harass the country. After passing this unusual place, the road drops down through turn after turn, until it enters a barren plain south of the city of Cheren.

For the first time we began to see camels. When you first become acquainted with camels, they give the impression of being creatures with a smug, bad-tempered disposition. They may appear stupid at first, but never forget, they can remember a fancied hurt or insult for a long time and will get even at the first opportunity, when the offender is off guard. They show their resentment by spitting in a persons face, a mess of green, half-digested grass which smells to high heaven.

These long-legged, gawky animals are ideal beasts of

burden for the hot, dry lowlands, as they are very hardy and will stand up under extreme conditions. They are valuable property in this part of the country. They are used as beasts of burden, are useful for the milk they give, their fine hair which can be used in the making of warm coats and even for their meat. The average camel will drink water every day, given the opportunity, but he can go for a week or more without water if necessary.

Riding a camel is a real sensation, for they are pacers. As a result they walk with a long, swinging stride which produces a rolling gait and has won for them the name, "ship of the desert." The effect they have on the novice is something like that produced by a rolling ship on a land-lubber, a good case of "motion sickness."

Two distinct types of camel are found in this area. The beautiful white camel is the riding camel and can travel up to a hundred miles in a day, outrunning a good horse on a long haul. The brown camel is the beast of burden, carrying a load of six hundred pounds on his back and covering twenty-five to thirty miles a day.

It is quite amusing to watch camels while they are being loaded. They moan and groan in protest, their big brown eyes rolling in a way that makes them appear to be sick. Once I saw an unhappy camel put on a bucking exhibition which would have made the average Western bronc "green with envy." He was most unhappy over having to carry a man on his back. As he rose from his huge, knobby knees, he literally came unjointed at all hinges, with long legs flying in every direction. The unfortunate rider was thrown head over heels, with his burnoose flying like the wings of some unusual type bird. He got up, spitting sand and full of Moslem oaths, which are really breathtaking if you understand them. After beating the big beast with a long stick, he tried again, only to have the same thing happen.

This went on for some time, the rider being thrown and the beast receiving a severe beating each time, until he finally decided he couldn't win the battle and gave in. Most of the nomad tribes of Africa count their wealth in the number of camels, goats, and cattle they possess.

The people of the Cheren Area are a distinct change from those seen at Asmara, fifty miles away. Here for the first time we saw the fierce tribesmen of the plains. They are lighter colored for the most part than their mountain brethren. The men have proud faces, set off by prominent hawk-like noses, thin lips, high cheekbones, and piercing eyes. Their women, contrary to Moslem custom in many areas, go unveiled and wear heavy silver bangles on their ankles and wrists and large gold nose rings. The men are tall, handsome fellows with fantastic hairdos and all carry curved daggers in their belts, which they will use at the slightest excuse.

It is not unusual to find a tribesman carrying one of the heavy, two-handed swords which may have come from some Frankish captive during the crusades. Some carry round shields made from the hide of the rhinocerous, which will turn a .30 caliber bullet fired at a hundred yards. Many are armed with long throwing spears which they can hurl fifty or sixty yards with great accuracy.

In spite of this step into the Middle Ages, Cheren is more famous for it's modern historical background. It was here in 1941 that British and Sudanese forces finally forced the Italian Army to stand and fight. Early one morning, the allied forces scaled the almost perpendicular cliffs which guard the city from the west. In the savage battle that followed, 3500 of the attacking force were killed, but they broke the back of Italian resistance in East Africa. These brave men lie buried in a little cemetery that overlooks the scene of their greatest triumph.

Cheren is one of the most picturesque little cities in East

Africa. Although the city lies in a bowl surrounded by mountains, it is still at an elevation of 3000 feet. This makes for a delightful semitropical climate; warm during the day and deliciously cool at night. The air in the city is scented from the groves of citrus fruits which flourish on the north side of town and by masses of tropical flowers that grow in profusion from nearly every available plot of unused ground.

The U.S. Army has a lovely little rest hotel here. Once the villa of an Italian general, it is now the "jumping-off" spot for most of the hunting parties who hunt the vast plain country of western Eritrea. We took time off to drink an ice cold lemonade, made from fresh lemons picked in the hotel gardens. It was time to begin shedding garments. Although it was only 7:30 in the morning, the bright sun had burned away the fog of the mountains and was shining down in what was to be the beginning of a beautiful day. We had scarcely drawn to a stop, when we were surrounded by scores of dirty, half-naked little tykes. There were a few beggars calling out, "Baksheeshi!" but most were merely curious.

Many Americans didn't like the Eritrean people, but I found them to be a happy, friendly folk. This was especially true when one got away from the larger towns and cities. It might also have had to do with my philosophy of life, when I travel about the world. I'm a firm believer in the saying: "To have friends, a man must prove himself friendly." I have never had this fail for me anywhere. Another thing that never ceased to amaze me was that the fierce desert tribesmen, with a fearsome reputation among the mountain folk, were more to be trusted than their more civilized city cousins.

After a brief stop, we headed west, down the almost perpendicular escarpment, for another 2,000 feet, to the floor of the plain which was still a thousand feet above sea level. At the 120 kilometer marker, we turned to the left on a small dirt road for the last and most hazardous lap of our trip. We had stepped in one turn from the civilized to the ancient, where men lived as they had for thousands of years.

Once you leave the hard-surfaced roads of Eritrea you are on dirt trails. Busses travel these so-called roads at regular intervals of several times a week, but by no stretch of the imagination can they be called roads. Many places the trail was so narrow that there was barely room for the truck and at times the jeeps had to back up several times in order to make it around a corner. There were no guard rails here, and the path dropped abruptly away for hundreds of feet to the floor of the valley far below. Usually the faint hearted dismounted at these times.

This was part of the vast veldt country of Africa, country that stretches for thousands of miles with scarcely a break. Small mountain ranges bisect it and ranges of volcanic hills appear at irregular intervals. We were now in the Monsura Valley, some seventy miles long by forty wide. There are no permanent type villages in this area, except for the village of Monsura itself, which is the center control point for the government of this large area. Occasionally we would pass native villages, which were usually the temporary villages of the nomads, with tents made from goat skins. Once in a while, the stone, mud, and straw-thatched hut of some farmer could be seen, surrounded by a bomba wall made from acacia thorn bushes and placed around the house as protection from the wild beasts. Most of the older boys and men were armed with spears or wicked-looking knives.

For those of you who have never traveled over a rough

road in a jeep, there aren't words enough to describe this bone-jarring experience. It seems as though every bump in the trail is transferred from the wheels of the little car through the stiff springs and unyielding seat cushions, to the base of the rider's spine. After several hours of this type of travel, it is almost impossible to stand erect when you first dismount.

To complicate things, add up the fact that the roads are not covered with fine gravel, as country roads are apt to be in the States. Instead they may be of solid rock, or of rock the size of a man's head. In areas where there is no rock, the consistency of the roadbed will match that of fine flour, which drifts around the slowly moving vehicles in a dense, stifling cloud and filters into everything. Mixed with perspiration caused by the fierce sun, it transforms the rider's face into grotesque caricatures. This dust is probably the worst hazard of safari travel in any part of Africa. During the rainy season, these dusty roads become quagmires of sticky red mud which engulf and hold tight to any vehicles unlucky enough to get in their grasp.

Many times it is easier to drive beside the road, as the plain may be as flat as a table top. This is complicated however by the fact that so much of the ground is covered with the tough thorns from the acacia bush. These are long and tough enough to pierce the fibers of an eight-ply combat tire and will easily penetrate the sole of a hunting boot. All vegetation in Africa seems to be antagonistic to human life. Grasses come equipped with saw-toothed edges and every plant seems to have either seeds or blades which cling to the body of man or beast like blood-thirsty leeches.

The noonday heat, even during the cooler seasons of the year, may climb to well over a hundred degrees; yet it is not as uncomfortable as might be expected, for there is almost no humidity. Because of this, it is very important for a person to wear a head covering during the hot part of the day to avoid sunstroke. It is also vitally necessary to take salt tablets to replace salt lost through perspiration. This is beneficial in halting heat prostration. It was from country such as this that the immortal words came: "Mad dogs and Englishmen, go out in the noonday sun." This is pretty much the truth, for most all the natives take a siesta period during the hottest part of the day.

Our progress was slow and sometimes we were forced to crawl along at a snail's pace. The trail had been criss-crossed with gullies washed in the surface by the fierce rains of the rainy season. We were the first vehicles to pass this way in a long time and were the first to do road maintenance since the roads washed away. Many times it was necessary to repair the shoulders of some steep gully that barred our forward progress. Other times, we had to stop and, using the cable on the truck, winch our way across a wet spot in the stream bed. At one place, too far for the cable to reach, we had to cut palm fronds and build a roadbed across the soft sand. It was hot, dry, difficult work, but no one seemed to mind too much. After all, we were nearing the hunting area and all that mattered to us was to get there as soon as possible.

Rounding the shoulder of a little hill, I saw my first African game animals. About 500 yards away, standing droop-hipped in the shade of a giant thorn tree, was a herd of eight Grant's gazelle. It is hard to imagine any animal being more beautiful and graceful than a member of the gazelle family. There are some sixty different kinds of gazelle in Africa. Most of them are small and very swift. Except for the first blinding burst of speed, many of the gazelle can outrun the cheetah. I have followed them across the flat

plains at sixty miles an hour on many occasions without
coming close to them.

The Grant's gazelle is in the middle bracket as far as size
is concerned. A large male will stand about 35 inches at the
front shoulders and weigh up to 150 pounds. The male has
long, lyre-shaped horns which may reach a length of thirty
inches and are ringed for their full length. The horns of the
female are shorter and slimmer. These animals travel in
herds of considerable size, sometimes numbering into the
hundreds. This seems to be a characteristic of most gazelle;
they are a very gregarious breed of animal.

They cross the plains in unbelievably long, graceful
bounds. It would be hard to imagine a more lovely sight.
Often they will race with a hunting car. They do not seem
to be frightened of vehicles and will run alongside and then
sprint in front of the car with a tremendous burst of speed.
When they are going all out, they will lay their heads along
their backs and clear the ground and any obstacles in their
path with tremendous leaps.

This herd was standing, heads alertly raised, as they
studied the intruders who had so suddenly appeared to disturb their siesta. As we looked through our binoculars, we
could see that three of the bucks had fine trophy horns.

I noticed Pat's jeep slide away from the convoy and head
in the direction of the herd. Even though I was a novice on
my first trip, I noticed he stayed downwind of the animals.

"Sarge she going to get camp meat," Cookie pointed out
unnecessarily. Stopping the vehicle about three hundred
yards from the animals, Pat and Rocky began a careful forward stalk, keeping clumps of thorn bushes between them
and their quarry. As long as the men were partially concealed, the gazelle did not seem to be particularly frightened.
When the hunters reached a point about 150 yards from the
animals, the bucks began to show their nervousness.

"Sarge she better damn well shoot now," Cookie kept saying over and over sotto voce. The bucks were tossing their heads up and down, while we could see their tails flick rapidly from side to side.

"Shoot, shoot," Cookie repeated over and over again, "she's going to dam run pretty soon."

As we watched, we heard the sharp bark of Rocky's little 25/20 and a fine buck leaped high into the air to drop kicking to the ground.

No sooner had the buck dropped, than Fadul motioned me to drive to the fallen animal. Even while we were still in motion, he leaped from the moving vehicle and knife in hand rushed to the downed animal to cut its throat.

"Why does he do that?" I asked Cookie. "Ah," said that staunch Coptic, "he's damned heathen, all Moslems must cut animal throat while still alive, or they cannot eat meat."

As I pulled up beside the fine animal, Fadul gave me a big grin.

"Now I can eat meat," he said. "This is called 'chingi' in our religion. We were ordered by the prophet to eat no meat unless it has been killed in this manner. Its throat must be cut while life is still in the body, or the meat is unclean."

"Why you no eat pig?" Cookie mocked at him. "You can cut pigs throat as well."

Fadul mumbled something in Sudanese which I was to find out later meant something about Cookie's mother being a camel and his father a hyena.

Fadul was always having words with Cookie over his religious observances. Although they were usually the best of friends, Cookie would tease the fat Moslem boy until he would lose his temper and chase Cookie about the camp, butcher knife in hand, screaming Moslem curses, while Cookie laughed.

Cookie especially made fun of Fadul's prayers. Five times

each day, at prescribed times, the Moslem got out his little prayer rug, unfolded it and, facing the Holy City of Mecca, he would say his prayers. His mournful cry of "Allahuk'bar-! A'shadadu la ilah il Allah; wa Mohammed er-rasool Allah!" (God is great! I testify there is no God but God and Mohammed is His Prophet), would send cold chills up and down my spine.

Rocky had killed a lovely trophy. The one-shot kill lay, with its golden hide shimmering in the sun like spun gold. The black and brown markings on its side blended into the white of its belly. The horns were almost perfectly matched, having twenty-three rings each.

"That's a mighty fine trophy for this area, son," said Pat. "Since it's your first trophy for Africa, what say we have it mounted?" Rocky was in full agreement. The fine animal had been dropped by a perfect shot through the near shoulder.

At fourteen, Rocky was a tall, stalwart, clean-cut young fellow. He had a cool head on his shoulders for a boy of his age and I liked to hunt with him. He was not one of the smart young ones who knew all the answers. He was willing to listen and learn from the experience of others. A fine friendship developed between us which was to last for the three years they remained in Eritrea.

In a matter of minutes, the expert hands of the two native boys had field dressed the buck and hung him in the back of the truck to cool. It never ceased to amaze me, the speed with which they could dress out an animal. Meat was always cooled of its body heat before putting it in the ice box, as this helped to preserve it. After the body heat had thoroughly left the carcass, it was carefully placed in the cooling box on a cushion of branches. This kept the meat from coming into direct contact with the ice and allowed air to circulate freely.

Even on a five-day hunting trip, where the noonday temperature might reach 115 in the shade, we seldom had meat spoil if it was properly taken care of. Many tasty roasts, steaks, and ribs were brought back by hunters, who kept the family deep freezes full most of the hunting season.

Shortly after shooting the gazelle, we reached the village of Mansura. It is only a collection of stone and mud huts, with one permanent type building that houses the police station. There are no modern conveniences and water is drawn from a communal well.

The police sergeant in charge of the little detachment told us there had been a great deal of shifta activity in the area. Only two days before, a party of Italian hunters had been attacked by a force of bandits estimated to number thirty men. One of the hunters had been badly wounded in a pitched battle. We were offered a police guard and two policemen climbed aboard my truck.

It was about two P.M. when we reached the banks of the Mansura River. We had been on the road for about eight hours and although we didn't know it, the worst of the journey was still ahead. At this time of the year, the river was dry. It was at least a mile wide at this point. During the rainy season, a torrent rushed down between its banks, tumbling huge rocks about as though they were toys. The force of the water could be clearly seen by looking at the debris which littered the banks. Huge palm trees had been uprooted and carried along by the fierce current. The sand in the river bed was white and fine, as nice as any on the finest seashore.

Both Pat and Eddie wanted to camp on the south side of the river. We started across. There had been no vehicular traffic at this point and we had no way of knowing how firm the river bed might be. The jeeps made it in fine style, but the truck, loaded as it was and pulling the heavy trailer, was a different matter. All went well until I hit a soft spot. Then before I realized what had happened, we were down to the axles in the fine sand. It was too far to shore for the cables to reach and we knew that the jeeps would not be heavy enough to help. There was only one thing to do: camp on the north side, while the truck with most of our supplies and the ice chest was left for the time being in the middle of the riverbed.

Setting up a hunting camp in Africa is simple, when you are not traveling deluxe safari style. It can be put up with less loss of energy than any camp I have ever been in. You set up your folding cot in the shade of one of the trees near the campfire. The mosquito net is suspended from a tree, or from sticks which are lashed together with twine. Open a folding chair and presto! your bedroom is ready for occupancy.

While we were laying out our personal gear, the boys were setting up the kitchen and gathering wood for the fire. Soon a huge, porcelain coffee pot was bubbling merrily on the fire, sending its tempting aroma around the camp area. This pot was never empty. You could come in any time of the day and find the hot, black coffee steaming over the fire. When you wakened in the frosty morning to the eerie cry of a hyena, it was to find a black, smiling face bending over your cot, with a steaming cup of coffee in his hand. You knew then that you were off for the start of a perfect hunting day.

Within a few minutes, the aroma of coffee was mingled with the tempting odor of sizzling gazelle steaks. The freshly killed meat was tender and delicious, with none of the wild flavor found in venison. Using his cooking wizardry, Fadul had broiled it until it could be cut with a fork. It was served with fried potatoes, gravy, and pans of hot biscuits which had been cooked in a heavy metal Dutch oven. I didn't realize how hungry I was, until I started in on my second huge steak.

After this fine meal, we sat around the area smoking and sipping on steaming cups of hot coffee, then went out to struggle over the mired truck. It was necessary to dig both the truck and trailer out of the sand, then build up the road-bed with palm fronds. The task was made more difficult because the truck and trailer had to be backed over the makeshift road.

By the time this was done, we were thoroughly "bushed." The day had been hot, possibly 110 degrees, but in the shade of the trees, a vagrant little breeze made it most enjoyable. When we got back to the camp area, we found a huge jug of ice cold lemonade which had been made by the ladies from fresh lemons purchased in Cheren.

Later that evening, as the sun began to sink behind the fringe of palm trees to the west, I took the two children and drove one of the jeeps down the river. The sand was packed as hard as pavement and you could speed along without raising a bit of dust.

Rounding a bend in the river, we surprised a large herd of baboons which had come down to water at a little pool that lay cool and inviting in the shade of a huge rock. The animals were of all sizes. Small babies rode piggy back on their mothers; grizzled males brought up the rear guard, while the startled herd began a mad dash across the river. Dismounting, I dropped a huge old male who had lingered behind. He would look mighty good mounted on the wall of my trophy room.

When the big animal dropped to the sand at the sound of my shot, I was surprised to see two others detach themselves from the fleeing herd, and come back to try and help their fallen leader. I watched in amazement as they tried to get him to his feet. When he would not get up, they tried to carry him. He was too heavy. Finally with a snarl that carried the deepest of hatred for me, they abandoned him and joined their fellows in the palm trees that lined the river bank.

They were making a terrible fuss, cursing and screaming at me in the very best-approved baboon fashion, calling down all sorts of baboon maledictions on me. My attention was focused on one big male. He would rush out into the riverbed, jump up and down, while beating himself on the chest and screaming at the top of his lungs. Then he would turn handsprings and run back on a palm log that jutted into the river. He was such a fine specimen I finally met his challenge to fight. I was a bit unfair though, I used a gun.

He fell behind a palm log and when I went to retrieve him, the other animals began to bombard me with sticks stones and small coconuts. With their big canine teeth bared, they rushed up to within twenty feet, as I dragged their fallen comrade back towards the jeep.

This was a case of "fools rush in where angels fear to tread." I knew no better. Later when I told of this experience, I realized how lucky I had been. Baboons worked into a sufficient frenzy, will attack anything. Their method of attack is to close with their victim and while holding it in their powerful arms, rend it with their teeth.

On a later hunting trip, I had occasion to come to the rescue of a companion who was being attacked by baboons. They had him surrounded in a little depression and were moving relentlessly in on him from all sides. Even though he had killed seven of them with his rifle, they were still out to finish him off. It was fortunate we heard his shots and were able to reach him in time.

That first night in our hunting camp was one of the strangest I ever spent anywhere. We were dead tired from the trip and especially from having labored over the truck. I was sure that after dinner, we would all "hit the sack." I was wrong. There is a ritual that is religiously followed in every African hunting camp I ever occupied. It usually starts with a pipeful of tobacco, or a cigar, to go with a steaming cup of coffee. Within seconds, the evening story-telling session is under full swing. As someone once said: "When this starts, the first liar doesn't have a chance." I guess this is true more or less wherever men hunt.

The coffee pot is bubbling. The thick, scalding brew is doubly delicious from having been made over an open fire. You are full of good food; the tobacco never tasted half as good before. Then the stories begin to come, thick and fast, each one funnier, or more ridiculous, than the other.

"Did you hear about the trouble they've been having with the mosquitoes at the Addis Airport? Seems like one of those big babies from the southern swamp country landed at the airport last week and before those damned WOGS could be stopped, they pumped him full of 1500 gallons of high octane gas."

Then someone recalled that the Ethiopian mosquitoes weren't so bad. He had been at an army camp in Louisiana he said, where they had diamond billed insects. A man working in his yard one night was attacked by a swarm of these vicious bugs and took refuge under a huge iron pot. As the insects bored their way through the kettle, he battered their beaks down with his hammer. This worked fine, until he captured several. They flew off with the kettle. The last they saw of the farmer, he was clinging to the bail of the kettle as they soared over the swamp.

One man came up with an amusing story about the em-

peror's return to Addis after the war. He landed at the new
air terminal and was received by a huge delegation of noble-
men. As he looked about, His Imperial Majesty noted the
many new buildings that had been built in his absence.
"Who built all these new buildings while I was gone?" he
asked. "The Italians, your Majesty," they replied. "If I had
known this," said the emperor, "I'd have stayed away a few
more years."

In what seemed like a few moments, the campfire had
burned down to a bed of glowing coals and the distant
thumping of drums from the native village across the river
had ceased. There is an almost unholy silence in the air.
You lay back, close your eyes, and before you know it you
are fast asleep.

With the sudden darkness of tropical night, the entire
character of Africa changes. The air becomes softer with
the approaching coolness. The stars seem to stand out in the
jet blackness of the night sky and are startling in their bril-
liance. It seems almost as though you could reach out and
pluck them from their ebony setting.

There is a subtle change on the ground too. Sounds become more acute. The slightest touch of metal on metal will
carry for a great distance and a campfire can be seen for
miles.

The animal kingdom wakes up too and joins in a cacophony of sounds that seems to erupt from nowhere. The dis-
cordant notes sound for all the world like some huge or-
chestra that is out of tune. In the trees overhead, guinea
fowl mutter sleepily as they are crowded on the roost. A
sleepy parakeet puts in his mumbled note of protest. The
great hornbill makes a sound like the pounding of a black-
smith on his anvil. The crickets and the tree frogs join in
to blend with the screeching, file-like sound made by the
hyrax.

Always you hear the baboons; not as noisy as during the day, but sounding off just the same in their usual irritable manner. Perhaps it is no more than a sharp bark of protest as they are crowded in their sleep, or it may be the insistent warning of some alert sentry who senses the stealthy approach of a leopard, or their greatest enemy the rock python.

As the night progresses, the sounds increase. Wart hogs can be heard fighting in the thick underbrush over the favor of some lady love. This sound mingles in some unknown way with the high-pitched cry of a nearby jackal. The barking of a herd of zebras drifts downwind to blend in with the harsh honking of a galloping herd of wildebeest. Sometimes the hunting cry of a leopard will be echoed by the coughing roar of the "king of the beasts." Always, you hear the spine-tingling scream of some animal which has fallen victim to one of the great predators. A constant battle for survival is going on out there all the time.

That first night on the African veldt will remain in my memory forever. Sometimes even now, years later, I wake during the night and recall the strange sensations that ran up and down my spine like icy fingers.

Sometime during that first night, you are shocked wide awake. There has been no sound, unless it was the snapping of a twig under the foot of some great animal out in the darkness. There is the vaguest hint of some strange, foreign odor in the air, but it is enough to make the short hairs on the back of your neck stand on end. The odor increases and you sit up and reach for your flashlight, realizing for the first time that your body is covered with goosebumps. You notice how low the camp fire has burned and how the sinister shadows have enroached on the camp area. They seem to be especially deep in the vicinity of your cot.

Suddenly without warning, from close at hand—so close

that it seems to come from the bushes next to your cot—a weird, moaning, sobbing cry commences that raises higher and higher to an ear-splitting crescendo and then dies away in a demented laugh. From the other side of the low fire comes an answering cry until you feel as though you are surrounded by lunatics. You hurry to the fire to pile on fresh wood from the nearby supply. As the flames leap higher, you see a circle of yellow-green eyes which glow back at you out of faces which might have come from one of Dante's nightmares. You think you are the only one awake. From a nearby cot comes a sleepy voice saying, "Go back to sleep! It's only those damn hyenas."

Our second night in camp, we discussed these unsavory animals in detail. Pat solemnly declared that a hyena will not kill a human being: "They will creep into camp however," he said without cracking a smile, "and bite a person's face off." Later that night the camp was shocked awake by an earsplitting scream which was definitely human. It came from the vicinity of Ellie's cot. I turned on my flashlight, to see one of the biggest, ugliest hyenas imaginable, sitting like a huge dog near the head of the frightened woman's bed. Later she swore that when she woke, it was to look into his face. "He was licking his chops," she sobbed on Eddie's shoulder. Her scream so unsettled the big dog-like creature, that he left camp at a shambling run, joined by several of his fellows who were lingering nearby. The whole tribe galloped away down the river bed, sounding for all the world like a herd of galloping horses. Ellie moved her cot closer to the fire and slept with her head towards the fire after that.

Breakfast in a hunting camp is one of the best times of the day. The morning is fresh and chilly; usually a jacket is welcome. You are wakened, most likely, by the singing of thousands of birds in the trees surrounding your camp.

If you are a heavy sleeper, one of the camp boys, will shake you awake and offer you a steaming cup of black coffee at the first sign of dawn in the eastern sky.

In the professional hunting areas of East Africa, such as Tanzania, Uganda, or Kenya, you will probably get a cup of hot tea, for the British influence is still strong there. Whatever it is, coffee or tea, it will be strong and hot and will bring you wide awake in seconds.

From the direction of the cooking fire comes the delicious aroma of bacon and eggs, to mix with the satisfying olfactory sensation caused by the bubbling coffee pot. You always eat good in a hunting camp. There is something about the air and the exercise that stimulates the appetite beyond imagination. If the bacon and sausage gives out in a couple of days, this can always be replaced by juicy steaks from the animals you have shot, or by the delicious breasts of guinea fowl or francolina.

Add to the meat, scads of eggs. No hunter leaves the camp area in the morning without at least six eggs under his belt. Top this off with piles of golden brown pancakes, fresh biscuits, and fruit. Wash it all down with about a gallon of scalding, black coffee and you are ready for whatever the gods of luck may decree.

After breakfast, pipes and cigarettes are lit, while final preparations are completed. Thermos jugs will be filled with cracked ice and water, with the juice of fresh lemons squeezed in for added flavor. There will be a last minute inspection of firearms. Ammunition will be distributed in the pockets of pants and jackets. Someone will re-check the gas and water in each vehicle, while another will make sure extra supplies are strapped on the rear of each vehicle. Then by two's or three's, you are ready for the day's hunting. Sometimes the gals will prefer to stay in the camp area, but don't be too surprised to return and find they have shot a better trophy than the men.

I recall one trip I went on with the Gilbert's and another girl. Janie and her friend remained in camp one day, while I took the men to a spot I knew, where the largest gazelle in the country usually hung out. Late that evening, worn to a nub from rough traveling over the African veldt, we made our sad and empty-handed way back to camp. Hanging from a limb in camp was one of the finest gazelle bucks I have ever seen. Janie had dropped him with one shot from her .270. For some reason the men were strangely quiet that night around the campfire.

We were not out for big game this trip, so were relying on light firearms and shotguns. In addition to the guineas and francolina, there were swarms of sand grouse and many turkey bustards. These big birds looked something like a crane, but tasted like wild turkey.

Most everyone carried a scoped rifle in .30 caliber, which was used for gazelle, hyena, baboon, and wart hog. Many of the telescopes were mounted on swing-away mounts, so you could change immediately from scope to iron sights if the situation warranted. This was of advantage in dense underbrush, where it was difficult to pick up a charging pig at close range in a scope.

The best hunting hours are in the early morning and late evenings. Then the animals are out in the open feeding, or on their way to and from some local water hole. The rays of the sun are much softer then and it is much pleasanter to hunt. In the middle of the day, there is real danger from sunstroke unless a person takes care.

Much of the hunting is done along the river bed, or around a water hole. During the dry season, these are often man made. The water hole we were camped near on our first trip was the only one within seventy miles. During the latter part of the dry season which usually ended the last of June, large numbers of animals could be found near these holes.

By nine in the morning, the rays of the sun are beginning to strengthen and they will push up to 100 or more by late afternoon. The air is dry, however, and a person is not en-nervated by humidity.

Noon on the African veldt, whether in the camp area or out under some thorn bush, has all the soothing softness of some lullaby. It seems as though all things that move and breathe fall under its spell. Here is one time in Africa, where there is a breathless silence. Without the aid of a watch, or the noon whistle from a local factory, you automatically know when it is noon. Both human and animal kingdom seem to be hypnotized; you seek the shade and open your lunch. A few hundred yards away, a herd of gazelle stand droop-hipped under an acacia tree, their heads hanging almost to the ground. You prop your back against the trunk of a tree, while a soft movement of the atmosphere, too gentle to be called a breeze, drifts across your face—the world floats along with it, leaving you, with your back against a tree and your hat in your lap, asleep. The last thing you hear before you drift off into dreamland is the soft chuckling of guinea fowl in the brush nearby or the restless barking of a herd of baboon in the trees near the river.

We were to see other members of the gazelle family on this trip: the oribi, which is the fastest runner of the smaller antelopes. When it is running from danger, but at a safe distance, it will spring high into the air, coming down on its hind legs first. It is a graceful little beast, usually moving in small groups and can be recognized by its yellowish brown color and the long tuft of hair at its knees. The male has straight ringed horns, about six inches long.

On several occasions, we saw one or two of the tiny dik-dik, a dainty little fellow which seldom stands over fourteen inches high, or weighs more than seven pounds. They are killed by the thousands every year and their hides used to make ladies' gloves.

This, then, is the story of a short hunting trip: up at break of day, hunt while the day is cool, siesta during the heat of the day and hunt again in the cool of the evening, or on stand at a water hole after dark.

Always we will remember those delicious moments, which will linger in our memory forever. Moments of complete peace with ourselves and the world; moments of meditation, when we are closer to God than seems possible; moments when we look at ourselves and are truly honest in our self-evaluation.

3 Robin Hood in Goatskins

During the hunting season of 1958, many complaints were directed against American servicemen for alleged violations of Eritrean hunting laws. These ranged from killing protected animals, to shooting in restricted areas and trespassing. Thorough investigation of every case was conducted by the Criminal Investigation Detachment at Kagnew Station and in a great majority of cases, the violations were found to have been committed by indigenous personnel and blamed on the Americans. However, evidence was found, indicating some type of control among American personnel would be desirable.

The commanding officer of Kagnew Station, Colonel Harris, was concerned with this situation. Every time an American serviceman was accused of a game violation, the colonel bore the brunt of displeasure from the State Department as exercised by the local American Consul in Asmara. Quite often this resulted in unfavorable pressure from higher military command.

The colonel was a fine sportsman in his own right and realized that unless this situation was alleviated immediately, it could very well cause the discontinuance of all hunting privileges for American personnel. Searching for some suitable solution, he asked the advice of his command.

This came as a real challenge to me. I had been interested in game conservation and sensible hunting laws for years. After a great deal of thought, I thoroughly discussed this problem with local hunters, both Italian and American. Then I visited many of the local chiefs in hunting areas and discussed the problem from their angle. Then armed with these facts, I sat down one evening to put my ideas on paper.

The necessity for stricter game-control measures had been brought home forcibly to me a few weeks earlier, when I had come across the rotting carcasses of over seventy wild pigs lying along a stretch of the Baraka River above the village of Hadundami. It appeared as though the animals had been slaughtered by someone who took sheer joy in killing. None of the delicious meat on any of the animals had been touched. On my own, I conducted an on-the-spot investigation and came to the conclusion that the animals had been shot by a party of Italians from the city of Agordat, some forty miles to the south. Local natives told me there were no Americans in the area when this incident took place.

I took time off from my hunting trip to drive back into the city and report the incident to the senior Eritrean game official. This got me into hot water, for already a story was being spread around the city accusing the Americans of the incident. The local game official tried to have me arrested and thrown into jail. Fortunately, I had made friends with the police chief. Through his efforts, I was able to get an investigation party to go back to the scene of the crime. There, with testimony of local chiefs staring them in the face, they had to admit the Americans were not to blame. As far as I can recall, the guilty parties were never brought to justice.

I was pretty unhappy about this incident, not only because of the treatment I had received from the officials, but also because I had lost a whole day from my three-day hunting trip. I managed to keep my feelings pretty well hidden and, as a result, eventually I developed a close and friendly relationship with the man who had tried to jail me.

From this incident came the idea of a game-enforcement system, operating within the framework of existing Eritrean law, but supervised and enforced by American personnel and dealing exclusively with Americans. Game wardens, operating under the control of the local provost marshal, would be appointed by the commanding officer. They would be authorized to inspect camp sites, hunting areas, hunting convoys, hunting licenses and game bags, to insure the game laws were being complied with. They would have the authority to arrest offenders if necessary and would, in addition, check on safety practices, both in the camp areas and on highways along which the hunting convoys rolled. When a game violation was reported through local officials, they would work closely with Eritrean officers to solve and apprehend the guilty party if he was an American.

Many of the local minor hunting laws had been disregarded by most everyone over the years. The Americans were as guilty as anyone in this respect. Many of these laws were of little value as far as game conservation was concerned, but they were important from a safety angle. One of the most frequently disregarded laws was one which forbade a hunter from shooting at any game from a vehicle, either moving or standing. The law stated that the hunter must dismount and move at least one hundred meters from the vehicle before firing at any game. This was a common-sense safety law and had been in effect for many years in most areas of East Africa, especially where the British had set up their superior systems of game control. Another frequently disregarded law was one which forbade a hunter to fire across any road, or within a hundred meters of any road.

There were other things that came to mind, too, during this period in which I was making my unofficial inquiry into the hunting situation. I noticed that there was a good deal of waste in use of government transportation to and from the hunting areas. Some of the beginners, many of them hunting for the first time in their lives, did not understand the operation of a military vehicle off a highway. Any one with experience will tell you that a jeep, for instance, which drives on the highway pretty much like a civilian type vehicle, is an entirely different breed of crittur' when driven on rough ground and in four wheel drive. This lack of knowledge had resulted in several rather serious accidents.

When I made my recommendations to the colonel, I suggested that along with the game-enforcement section, consideration be given to setting up base hunting camps which would be operated by personnel from Special Services. This system would economize on transportation and gasoline consumption. Each of these hunting camps would be self-contained, with enough equipment to take adequate care of a hunting party of eight people for a five-day period. The hunter would furnish his own personal gear such as blankets, food, and ammunition.

Each camp was provided with two native guides who could be hired for the sum of 25c U.S. per day. Two jeeps were available for transportation at each camp and were to be used within the hunting area only. Gasoline was furnished for these vehicles at the cost of 18c per gallon. The camp boy and cook were paid the equivalent of $1 U.S. each per day.

We figured the average hunting party to have a maximum of six hunters, although we could take care of up to eight. Under the conditions planned on, this party could hunt for five days from this semi-permanent camp, in reasonable comfort. They would have few worries other than bagging their game and this could be enjoyed for a cost of less than $2 per day, bargain prices no matter how you look at it.

Every five days, a truck loaded with supplies and ice, pulling a 450 gallon water trailer would leave Kagnew Station with a hunting party. On the return trip, they would bring back the successful hunters and their meat. It was not unusual for a party of six men to bring back 3,000 pounds of meat. This was worth much more than the cost of the trip. Nearly every American family at Kagnew Station had a deep freezer for storage of this meat.

The system of hunting out of a fixed camp served a two-fold purpose. First, it was much easier to check on hunters and game conservation when you knew exactly where the hunters were located. Second, each camp was under the supervision of a competent non-commissioned officer, who was responsible that proper safety precautions were observed within his camp area at all times. Immediately this went into effect, the percentage of hunting accidents fell drastically. Another advantage of these camps was that it allowed the beginner the chance for success. Before this, many men went into the country on their first hunting trip, many of them came back empty handed for they did not know where to hunt. Hunting from our camps, which were located in three of the best hunting areas, a man had a better than even chance of being successful. These camps were moved periodically so that game would not become depleted in one area.

Colonel Harris was pleased with the plan. After a lengthy discussion, he asked me who would make a good game warden. I put in a good word for myself and got the job.

After a discussion with army authorities, I purchased a new British Land Rover for use on the job. This four wheel drive vehicle is similar to the jeep, except it is a bit larger, much more stable on rough ground, and a good deal more comfortable to ride in. It is by far the most popular safari vehicle in Africa and has proved its value over the years. The army was to reimburse me for traveling expenses at the rate of 5c per mile spent on official business.

To add to the serviceability of the vehicle, I added a 60-gallon water tank, a 40-gallon auxiliary gasoline tank, and an ice box which would hold ice enough for a five day trip. There was plenty of room on top of the ice box for two men to sleep in comfort. This was handy, as it eliminated the necessity of carrying a tent for inclement weather. When the weather was nice, we usually slept beside the truck on folding cots.

One of the more difficult aspects of the new job was the drafting of a set of rules to govern hunters while in the field. I made a special trip to Nairobi, Kenya, British East Africa, where I talked at length with veteran officials of the game-enforcement department. These men had the benefit of many years of game enforcement experience and of dealing with the hunting public. I found them to be most helpful and cooperative.

When the new system went into effect, hunters leaving Kagnew Station were required to submit a written request to the provost marshal at least thirty days before their planned trip. In the case of enlisted personnel this request had to be counter-signed by their commanding officer. Each party was required to be under the supervision of a man with at least the rank of sergeant. The senior man was responsible for the actions of his party and for their safety on the trip.

The hunting request contained vital information pertaining to dates of the hunt, camp area to be used, number of persons by name, age and rank, types of weapons they would be carrying, with identifying serial numbers and identifying numbers of hunting licenses. All paper work was handled by the provost marshal's office. Locations of each group were posted on a large map of the area kept for this purpose in the guard house and each party was required to sign out on leaving the area and sign in on returning.

These restrictions may seem to be a bit aggravating. They were necessary for the safety of the hunting party. Armed bandits, known as "shiftas," wandered over large areas of Eritrea. Many of these men were holdovers from World War II, where they had been armed and trained by the British to fight as guerrillas against the Italians. When the war ended, they found it more profitable to rob than to work for a living. Many of these men had gathered together in bands, some of considerable size and were a constant threat to anyone coming into their area of operation.

Few Americans left the city limits of Asmara unarmed. Some hunting parties, leaving for the field, looked like modern versions of the old covered wagon trains that crossed our western plains. I have made many trips into the hinterlands of Eritrea, sitting beside a driver with a shotgun loaded with 00 buckshot in my lap.

American vehicles or hunting parties were seldom molested by these bandits. Whether it was due to the fact that they held Americans in higher regard than others, or that most Americans were armed and were willing to use their weapons, is a moot question. Many of the bandit attacks on hunting camps were for the purpose of obtaining arms and ammunition. As a result, if a man lost a weapon on a hunting trip, it was considered mighty serious and he was in for trouble with both American and Eritrean officials.

During the five years I was in Eritrea, there were only five attacks that I can remember against Americans. In every case, the bandits came out "holding to the short end of the stick." My boss, the Provost Marshal, was in one of the more serious attacks. His hunting camp near the Ethiopian-Sudan border was attacked one night by about twenty armed men. The three American hunters, aided by their wives, beat off a three-hour attack that left three enemy dead. The Provost Marshal had his arm shattered by a bullet from a British Enfield rifle.

Possibly the best-known incident involving these land pirates and American personnel took place in the spring of 1959. An army truck loaded with mail was on its way from the Red Sea port of Massawa to Asmara. A few miles outside the city of Asmara, it was ambushed by eight heavily armed bandits. While they were in the process of looting the truck, an escort jeep with two men drove up behind the truck. Five of the bandits ran to intercept the jeep and were met with a withering blast of fire from the guards submachine guns. Two of the bandits fell. The others ran. As they scattered among the cactus growing beside the roads, the guards dropped two others with their fire.

In the meantime, the three men left behind at the truck opened fire on the escort with their rifles. This brief respite gave the truck driver the opportunity he had been waiting for. He got his weapon into operation and when the smoke had cleared, four of the bandits lay dead and another was seriously wounded. The next day, police searching the mountain side found the body of another, who proved to be the much-wanted leader of a local band. After this battle, in which the Americans came out without a scratch, it was a long time before the shiftas opened fire on any vehicle bearing the Stars and Stripes. It is only fair to say here, the hero of this mountain battle was a navy man.

Not many Americans had the chance to meet a shifta face to face and few cared for this dubious privilege. I met one in the Mansura Area—one of their strongholds—shortly after I got into the Game Warden business.

The local police chief warned me that there were many bandits in the area.

"The shifta chief has at least 350 armed men under his command," the officer told me. "They have an unsigned truce with the police. To be honest with you, we do not have enough men to control them. Only the army is strong enough to venture into their area and they will not cooperate with us."

The first night in that area, we set up camp. It was dark. The camp fire was burning cheerily, when seven heavily armed men slipped into camp without a sound, appearing as though by magic. Our native boys were almost hysterical with fear and kept mumbling something to the effect of "give them anything they want, or we will all be killed."

These men were as tough looking as I have ever seen. Dressed in old cast-off British Army uniforms and armed to the teeth, they looked mean and formidable. The only good sign I could see was a twelve-year-old boy who was with them.

I greeted them cordially enough, trying to hide signs of the nervousness I felt. We served them gallons of hot, black tea, sweetened with much sugar. This was their favorite beverage. They sat cross-legged around the fire for a long time without saying a word. The tension built up with each passing moment.

Their leader was a man who could have been anywhere between the ages of thirty and sixty. He was an imposing figure, standing over six feet tall; handsome in a savage sort of a way; with piercing black eyes that seemed to look into a man's soul. He was clean shaven, while most of his men wore heavy beards. His face and forehead were covered with dark blue tribal scars. The outfit he wore would have been more interesting to me if the tension had been less. It was a gaudy dress which was made up of a red velvet vest and a black coat, fitted over a suit of fine chain mail which must have been hundreds of years old and which no doubt had one time belonged to some Christian knight during the crusades. The bottom part of his costume was made up of baggy pants, which were fastened at the ankles over fine kid sandals. They were of brilliant purple silk. Unlike the rest of his men, he did not wear a turban. His hair was set in a fantastic coiffure, with the handle of a wooden comb protruding from its bushy mass. He was heavily armed, carrying a British-Enfield rifle with criss-crossed bandoleers of ammunition across his chest. Into the wide leather belt that spanned his waist were thrust two Webly revolvers and two curved-bladed, wicked looking knives. He identified himself as the local chief. The boy was the youngest of his many sons.

Using the frightened Fadul as an interpreter, I talked with this imposing figure of a man.

"I have brought my son to you because he has a sick finger," he said.

Then he lapsed into a language that seemed familiar but

which I could not place at the time. Then I suddenly remembered it was Swahili. I had heard it in Kenya many months before. It was sort of a universal language that is used among many tribes in East Africa. This was the first time I had heard it used this far north.

"Toto, m'boya sana," he said as though in resignation. Fadul did not understand, but Cookie's eyes lighted with reconition.

"I know what he speaks, sarge," he said, "it is the language called Swahili."

"I know he is talking about his son, because I heard him use the word 'toto' which means little one, but what else did he say?"

"He say the boy is very bad sick."

"Ask the man how his son got hurt," I said.

After a long conversation, I found that the boy had driven a thorn into his finger several days before. When it began to fester, the local doctor was called and had bound up the infected finger in a concoction of camel manure.

"That shenzi," the chief said fiercely under his breath, "ah wei-wei nasima rongo."

"He say, 'that rude savage (his doctor)' tell him many lies and say his boy be okay. Now he very mad because his boy bad sick."

I looked closely at the little fellow. When I placed my hand on his forehead I didn't need a thermometer to tell that he was burning up with fever. He was a very sick little boy.

I examined the patient closely. His arm was badly swollen to the shoulder, with angry red marks shooting up the arm. When I felt under his armpit, I found a hard lump which I knew was a bad sign.

"Tell this man I am not a hakim (doctor)," I told Cookie.

When the father was told, he shrugged his shoulders in the fatalistic manner of the people of the Near East and said:

"Shun ya nungu."

"What does he say."

"He says, 'now it is an affair of God.'"

"Do the best you can," Fadul whispered, then he too shrugged his shoulders and murmurred, "Inshallah!"

"What in the world are you mumbling about?" I asked.

"I only say, 'it is the will of God.'"

So I operated on my first patient. I had no special medical training other than normal first aid taught in the army, but I did have a good supply of first aid materials at hand and through the use of good common sense and a bit of luck I felt I could do a better job than the local hakim. I knew the job I was undertaking might have serious consequences if I failed, but the boy would surely die if nothing was done for him and this overshadowed any fear I had at the time.

As I began to soak away the evil smelling bandage I breathed a prayer to my God that everything would be okay. I knew Fadul was praying to the Prophet and was sure Cookie was doing his spiritual best to help. Looking at the evil face of the father, I knew that my best skill was needed, for I could visualize a cut throat if anything went wrong.

It was necessary to lance the boy's finger and lay it open to the bone. I could see grave problems in doing this, as I had no pain killer. He took the operation without flinching, as I opened the finger to the bone and scraped away as much of the infection as possible. One of my hunting companions helped as an assistant until we reached this stage. Then suddenly he excused himself and went off behind some bushes, where he made strange retching sounds.

The patient watched the operation with detached interest.

I trimmed away the infected flesh with a pair of scissors and doused the finger with a liberal application of sulfa powder. The incision was sewn up with a darning needle, using monofilament fishing line. When I finished, I gave the boy some sulfa tablets with instructions how to use them. His father thanked me gravely and left with his entourage. We breathed sighs of relief.

Early the next morning, Cookie rushed to wake me. "They come back," he panted in his fear. I picked up my double shotgun and making sure it was loaded with buckshot, I leaned it against a tree where it was in easy reach and waited to see what they wanted. As they came closer, I noticed that several of the men were carrying chickens with their legs tied and one had a basket of fresh eggs.

"My son is much better today," said the smiling father. When he smiled it completely changed the character of his face. "I sent him out to herd camels today. Truly your medicine is strong and your heart is good."

Even though I was a Christian, I was able to say with no hypocrisy: "Inshallah! It is God's will."

He insisted on leaving an armed guard so none of his tribe would molest us. From that day on, I was received with honor every time I visited his area. He would travel for miles to visit my camp and would always bring gifts of eggs, chickens, and fruit. We became good friends.

One day, as I came into his village, which was nothing more than a temporary encampment of goatskin tents, he met me with the typical greeting of friends in this area—the embrace. This was a bit hard to take at first, as the handsome fellow had been away from soap and water for a long time and smelled pretty raunchy. He said he had prepared a feast in my honor, which was to be held in his tent that night. It was a most unusual feast.

I have attended banquets all over the world; in the mountain villages of Japan; on the islands of the Yellow Sea; in farm homes of Korea; in adobe houses in Old Mexico; in Eskimo huts above the Arctic Circle. None was to equal this.

The meal had been cooked outside and was served in the largest of the conical, goatskin tents. There were ten men present beside Fadul and myself. The heat was stifling, the smell of unwashed bodies overpowering. Others present were the chief and nine of his lieutenants. We sat cross-legged on goatskin rugs and drank fermented mare's milk from gourd jugs.

Finally, after elaborate ceremonies, the evening meal was served. First a loaf of unleavened bread was brought into the tent. The chief broke this into twelve fragments and gave a piece to each guest. These bread fragments were dipped into a dish of salt. It was the ages old custom of breaking bread and sharing salt with a man. A custom which in this part of the world means that you are his friend and have his protection as long as you are under his roof.

The main course of the evening was carried in on a huge brass tray which took four men to bear. On the beautifully embossed tray lay a whole roast camel. The camel had been stuffed with a young heifer; the heifer was stuffed with a calf; the calf with a goat; the goat with a kid; the kid with a chicken; and the chicken was finally stuffed with a dove. Each bird and animal had been surrounded by highly spiced rice and vegetables. The whole conglomeration had been roasted over coals in a pit for two days. It smelled delicious and tasted even better.

Before arriving at the feast, Fadul had given me a brief-ing on the proper etiquette to use. As a result I did not make some of the embarrassing mistakes which are often made by Americans eating with Moslem hosts for the first time.

"There will be no eating utensils on the table," Fadul said. "You will use your hunting knife to cut the meat. Do this with your left hand and carry the meat to your mouth with your right hand. When you eat the rice, you will also use your right hand."

"Why is this?" I asked.

"You do not know?" asked the Sudanese boy, "ah you Christians are strange ones. It is because the left hand is un-clean. It is an insult if you carry food to your mouth with this hand."

"Who's strange?" I growled. "What's wrong with using your left hand to eat with?"

"Very strange indeed," he said, shaking his head. "You use your left hand to handle yourself when you piss don't you? This makes it unclean."

The feast went on without a hitch. The food was delicious and I found myself cramming it into my mouth with as much gusto as the other members of the party. When you got a handful of hot rice you had to act fast or your fingers were burned, as a result, the action at the table would have been the envy of Henry VIII. I ate until I felt as though I would burst. There were no cloths for cleaning the greasy hands; you merely licked off your fingers and wiped the rest of the grease on your pants. I followed suit. The savory food was washed down with copious draughts of the fermented camel's milk. I didn't realize at the time, but this mixture is flavored by the addition of fresh cows blood, urine, and wood ashes. I can't say it was one of my favorites, even without this knowledge. Fortunately, I have a cast-iron stomach and suffered no after effects.

Another custom that intrigues me is the manner in which you show your appreciation for a fine meal. After the final wiping of fingers, you sit back with a look of satisfaction on your face, rub your belly, and belch as loudly as possibly. This is accompanied by saying: "Al' ham' dul'lillah." (For the blessing of God.) The louder a man belches, the happier his host becomes, for this shows he has clearly enjoyed his meal. With a belly full of the rich meat and urine-flavored camels milk, there were some amazing belches. For a novice, I didn't do half bad myself.

Although the feast was held after sundown and it was cooling off outside, inside the tent it was still hot. The heat was not as bad as the smell. As perspiration trickled down the faces of the guests, I noticed it was streaked with grease from their hair.

"It is the hair you smell," whispered Fadul, noticing my discomfort.

From outside the tent came the strident call of a man's voice:

"Bal-ak! Bal'eek! Bal-ak! Bal-eek!" it said, "Make way! Make way!"

The flap of the tent was raised and a bedouin dancing girl undulated her way into the tent. The guests began to clap their hands, as musicians materialized and began to play the savage, mournful strains that have been the music of the desert people for time immemorial.

The girl was young, probably not over fourteen or fifteen, but she had the body of a mature woman. She was as graceful as a gazelle. A filmy veil partly covered her face, which was like engraved ivory. Her jet black hair fell to her waist like the wings of a raven. Her shapely arms were covered with silver wristlets, while around her delicate ankles, above her bare feet, were bangles that sounded like little silver bells as she danced. Her body, a golden brown, was only partially concealed under a gauzy jacket and flowing trousers. It was full blown and enticing. Her face was as finely chiseled as some Egyptian princess, with the large almond-shaped eyes peculiar to the desert women. Her dance was a dance of pure lust which had the guests licking their lips in anticipation within a few moments of her entrance. It might have come direct from the devil's repertoire. When she passed close to me, as she did quite often, since I was the guest of honor, her postures were definitely lewd and inviting. Any feelings that might have been stirred by her lascivious dance were quickly dispelled when she got close to me. "Whew" Someone needed to tell that little gal about deodorant and mouthwash!

Following the dancing girl were two stalwart fellows, who, naked to the waist, did a complicated dance with heavy, two-handed swords. It looked as though they were trying to hack each other to pieces. The musicians were good, I guess. At least they made up for their lack of rhythm, in frenzy and volume.

To top off the evening's entertainment, two completely naked giants stalked into the tent and wrestled. They were huge, burly men with bulging muscles and must have weighed close to three hundred pounds each. Their bodies had been rubbed with some evil-smelling grease, which made it hard for the opponent to get a handhold. They seemed bent on killing each other and the match did not end until one of them was carried senseless from the tent. The audience followed each movement of the match with bloodthirsty cries. There was nothing civilized about the performance. Somehow it reminded me of the cries of an American audience watching a boxing match at Madison Square Garden.

One thing about these desert men was of special interest to me and this was their elaborate coiffures. My host was delighted to tell me about them.

"They are a sign of rank among our men," he said. He went on to tell how each man vies with his fellows to produce the finest hairdo. First the head is washed with cow's urine to rid it of vermin. Following this, the hair is plastered with an aromatic gum mixed with camel manure. This is worked into the long hair, until it assumes the shape of a fantastic halo, offering all sorts of challenges to the individual barber. The hairdo is then dried in the sun and will last for weeks as long as it is kept out of the rain. It is similar to the hairdos found among the warriors of southern Sudan. These men were given the nickname of "Fuzzy Wuzzies," by the British and were memorialized in verse by the great British writer, Rudyard Kipling. Shaped in waves, halos, flat, or spread sideways, this hair style is the matter of great importance to each man. He protects it while sleeping by using a wooden block, much as that used by the Japanese geisha.

If you enjoy unusual odors, just try getting a couple of these fellows in a vehicle with you sometime, when the sun is boiling down at 120 degrees. The oil and manure mixture runs down their cheeks, to mix with the odors of bodies that have been unwashed for months. It is a potent mixture that you want to keep down wind.

4 Baboons Ain't People

A great deal has been written and spoken about the theory of evolution. Religious beliefs aside, I don't believe I descended from an ape. I realize, when you watch the antics of the great apes for some time, there is often a striking resemblance to human behavior. I have seen some people who resemble apes too and, in a comparison of behavior, I'm afraid the apes would have more reason to have their feelings hurt if this theory were true.

All members of the ape family will act like humans on occasion and most of them are remarkably intelligent. There are many natives in Africa who believe the baboon is human, or contains the spirit of some dear departed friend or relative. Because of this belief, baboons become pests in many areas. The natives will not drive them away from their fields or kill them. After all, would you be mean enough to deny your dear departed uncle a good meal?

When a herd of these animals drifts into an area and begins to destroy the crops, the native shrugs his shoulders and says: "Allah Inshallah!" (It is God's will, or what is written is written.) You hear this fatalistic phrase wherever

Moslem influence is felt. It is one of the things which has caused the people to remain backward. If anything bad happens to a person, it is God's will. If a friend is trampled by a rogue elephant, don't feel too bad about it, nothing could have been done about it for it was written that this should happen. If a child dies from some disease, if a man stumbles over a log and breaks his leg, if a cow is eaten by a crocodile, it is "Inshallah", God's will. If a woman is carried off by a hyena, or a man dies from snake bite, it is God's will. Few natives have the courage to remove the cause of the disaster.

Baboons are among the most destructive creatures I have even seen outside of man. In many parts of Africa, including Ethiopia, they are classified as vermin and can be shot at anytime. As far as I could make out, they are good for absolutely nothing other than for moments of amusement or extreme frustration.

A herd of baboons will often act like a gang of juvenile delinquents on the loose and will tear things up "just for the fun of it." They are like bad boys in a melon patch. Not satisfied with stealing a few melons, they must pull up the vines and break open the ripe fruit. I have seen them tear the fruit of banana trees off the branches to throw at each other, or to trample underfoot.

In spite of this, they are extremely interesting animals to watch and are among the most comical animals on the face of the earth. Africa would not be Africa without the huge herds of baboons which roam over most of its surface.

The gray baboon, sometimes called the Hamadryas, is the most common variety found in northern Ethiopia. He is a powerful animal which will stand close to four feet tall when full grown and may weigh as much as a hundred pounds. The male is very strong, with long muscular arms and long, sharp, canine teeth. Their method of combat is to close with their adversary, hold it in their arms and tear it to pieces with their teeth. In the northwestern part of Ethiopia, you may be fortunate enough to see a herd of black baboon. These are even bigger than their gray cousins, standing as tall as a man.

Most baboons are polygamous having as many as seven wives. Unlike some males of the human species, he will not share his wives and will beat them to death if they dally with another male. He will not be averse to stealing another female, however, if he is big and tough enough to get away with it.

It is rare to see two baboons in single combat. Usually baboon fights are battles royal which start between two big males over some female. One shows his teeth and begins to beat on the ground and on his chest, while he screams himself into a battle frenzy. Soon, others join the melee and often the poor female is torn to pieces by the combatants.

There are many ways in which they imitate humans. They tend to congregate in groups where they have definite leaders. Usually these are the wise oldsters, although not always the largest males. These old fellows seem to exert the same influence on their herd which native patriarchs exert on their families. Usually, though, the herd leaders are the large powerful males who are torn and scarred by many combats, maybe missing an ear, or with scars over their bodies. They peer out at the world from under beetling brows, giving the impression of age and wisdom.

In the family circle, it is not unusual to see a male and female walking together, with the male circling his mate's waist in a hairy embrace. The adults play with their babies much as human parents would.

When the troop is traveling, the leaders will usually be

in the front, while the largest of the young males make up the rear guard. Often the bachelors will travel in a troop by themselves.

They are easy animals to tame and make amusing pets when they are young. As they grow older, they tend to become dangerous, due mostly to their ungovernable temper which erupts for most any reason. When they are in the throes of these anger fits, they are very unpredictable. They are not the cleanest animals in the world and need a lot of care.

There have been some famous tame baboons. One of these was the pet of a South African railroad signalman. When his master was crippled in an accident, this baboon was taught to sweep out the signalman's shack, carry water, and do other simple chores. When the engineer of an approaching train blew his whistle, the trained animal would take him the key, which would unlock the watertower. This animal labored faithfully for his master for ten years until he died from tuberculosis.

In one of our hunting camps, we found a baby which had evidently fallen from his mother's back while they were being chased by some enemy. He was so tiny we had to feed him from a bottle, using the finger of a rubber glove as a nipple. He would hold his bottle and suck up the solution of dried milk and sugar, while his wrinkled little face looked for all the world like a little shrivelled old man who had not shaved in a long time.

When I first found him, he made no attempt to escape, he clung to me with little cries of delight, as though I was his mother. Possibly the fact that I had been in the brush for two weeks without a bath might have given him this idea, for I certainly wouldn't have passed any bodily sweetness tests. Whenever someone tried to take him away from me, he would cling to my shirt with a death grip and cry like a little baby.

As he grew older, he became badly spoiled. He was like a little child who always gets his way and who has never had applied psychology used on his seat of learning. He loved to eat sugar, but was not content to eat it from his dish. Instead he wanted to reach into the sugar bowl with his grubby little fist. The first time I caught him doing this, I smacked his fingers. Immediately, he threw himself on the ground, where he proceeded to throw a tantrum, screaming at the top of his squeaky little voice and pounding on the ground with his fists. For hours afterwards, he would have nothing to do with me. When I called to him, he would turn his back in injured dignity. I couldn't entice him with tidbits he usually loved. Eventually, in his own good time, he forgave me and came to nestle in my arms as I sat before the camp fire.

He was nicknamed "Little Haile" and stayed with us for one hunting season. He was an interesting addition to the camp. One of his favorite pastimes was to wrestle with the fellows, making ferocious noises and grabbing their hands with his teeth. He never bit deep enough to break the skin, although sometimes he would become a bit overly enthusiastic and deal you a mighty strong buffet. One day, he fell in love with a girl baboon from a passing herd and went off with her to take up housekeeping in the rocks. We saw him occasionally in the distance, but he never came back.

I spent many fascinating hours watching these animals at work, at play, and at lovemaking. They are among the most alert of all animals and it is difficult to get within gun range of them. Usually they have sentries posted on some high rock or in a nearby tree. If you are carrying a gun, they will stay away from you, but with a camera, which they seem to understand is different, you can get quite close. Sometimes one of the big males would object to being disturbed and would stalk stiff legged towards me, muttering bad words under his breath. Sometimes a young animal would try and come closer, only to have his mother cuff him a mighty clout alongside his head and send him howling into the rocks.

The lookouts always seemed to be on duty, whether the herd was on the move, at a water hole, or in the sleeping area. If danger approached, they would bellow out a warning which would send the females and young scurrying for safety, while the big males would converge on the danger point. Woe betide the leopard who let his taste for baboon get the better part of his judgment, for two or three males were more than a match for the hungriest leopard.

After a little experience, you could listen to the baboon talk and almost understand what they were saying. I would almost venture to say they had a language of sorts.

One day, following an old male, I tried to get within shotgun range of him. He was a magnificent specimen. When I first approached, he sat on his haunches, watching me. Every few seconds, he would give a sharp, short bark as though to say: "What is this strange-looking fellow doing here?" He was perfectly calm until I got within fifty yards. Then he got up and sauntered after the rest of the herd, looking back over his shoulder to see if I would follow.

I sat down on a rock to rest and he sat too. Not once did he give any indication that I was following. This went on for some time, when I suddenly jumped up and tried to close the distance with a burst of speed. He ran away from me at full speed for about a hundred yards. This time when he stopped he gave me the full treatment. He flung himself into the air, doing handsprings, screaming and beating his chest, while he howled for all the world to hear that I was a "dirty yellow coward." He flung every dirty baboon word at me he could remember, telling me in the meantime what he would do if he ever got his hands on me. He was so funny, I began to laugh and left, leaving him the victor.

When traveling undisturbed, the old men of the herd will often move along in single file, their shoulders humped forward and the knuckles of their hands brushing the ground. The females take a great deal of interest in their children and carry the little ones around on their backs while they search for food. They turn over rocks with their strong hands, looking for grubs and when they come to a rotting log, will tear it to pieces. If the log is too heavy for one to move, several animals will get together and lift it.

There is always a lot of noise around a baboon herd. Either they are chatting among themselves, or they are barking at some real or imaginary enemy. Sometimes the young will scream from the sheer exuberance of being alive.

One day, I chased a small herd up a steep mountain side and suddenly found myself among some overgrown boulders. I was moving carefully, for it was in places like this one was most apt to come on a snake. I stopped beside a huge rock the size of a house, when I noticed how very quiet it was. I was a bit worried, for the apes are like children. When they are quiet, they are apt to be up to some deviltry. I tossed a good-sized rock over the big boulder. That was the wrong thing to do, for immediately, a shower of rocks came hurtling back at me. This rock-throwing contest went on for some time and seemed to be good clean fun, until one the size of a baseball bounced off my shoulder. I beat a hasty retreat, leaving the tribe screaming in triumph from the top of the boulder. They knew superior marksmanship had won the day.

The two creatures most feared by the baboon are the leopard and the rock python. Neither of these will attack in the presence of the herd, but are always on the lookout for strays. The big snakes will sometimes creep up on the sleeping areas at night and try and pick off an unwary animal, while the leopard is always on the lookout for a baboon that has wandered away from the herd. Sometimes vicious battles are fought between leopards and the big baboons. Usually in single combat, the leopard will win.

Baboons are annoying when you are trying to stalk other game in the vicinity, for they are natural "tattletales." They often sit off to one side and watch the show. When you think you are within gun range of your quarry, they will shout until the alerted animals move out of danger.

They can be of help too. If a person becomes lost in the vastness of the veldt, they will lead you to water and any fruit or root they eat is edible for a human. When feeding, they often wander around in little groups. When one succeeds in finding food, he will notify the others and there is a general rush to see if he is telling the truth. They made life on the veldt amusing and provided many hours of amusement.

5 Hyenas in My Bedroom

The hyena, or "fisi" as he is called in the Swahili language, is one of the strangest animals God placed on earth. His looks and disposition can't be equalled by any other of the animal kingdom. Yet, in spite of this, unlike the baboon, the hyena seems to have a definite place in the great plan of nature; as they go about their business of being nature's garbage disposal units, they even resemble a human garbage collector with their disreputable looks and bad smell.

As late as 1960, hyenas wandered in the streets of the Ethiopian capital city of Addis Ababa, cleaning up garbage that was dumped on the curbs each night. It was not unusual during an evening of travel in the suburbs to see as many as forty or fifty of these ungainly animals.

Regardless of its amusing appearance, a full grown hyena is no animal to fool around with. The spotted, or laughing hyena, as he is sometimes called, is the largest and most common of the breed found in East Africa. A big male will stand three feet at the front shoulders and weigh as much as 175 pounds. Some experts say they have the strongest jaws in the animal kingdom and they will get no argument from me, for I have seen them crunch through the thigh bone of a large ox with one bite. Often they will devour a dead animal—hide, bones, guts, and even the skull.

One night, I watched four of them work on the carcass of a large zebra stallion we had shot that day. Snuffling, grunting, and moaning, they had the carcass stripped to the bone within twenty minutes. By morning, there was nothing left to show for the night's feast except a trampled place in the grass and some blood stains.

Several times, I had a box seat at demonstrations of their strength. One night, we wounded a big male and drove up to put him out of his misery. He had been hit in the hind quarters and partially paralyzed. As the crippled animal dragged himself towards the vehicle, growling horribly, he bit into one of the eight ply combat tires, tearing out a sizeable chunk. That is a pretty hefty bite no matter how you look at it.

Although extremely powerful, this animal is seldom aggressive and has earned the reputation of being a confirmed coward. He will seldom attack anything alive, unless it is weak, or wounded so badly it can't protect itself. One night, two American soldiers, driving their sports car on the highway south of Asmara, overturned on a sharp curve. One of the men was knocked unconscious and pinned under the car. His friend went for help. When we arrived some two hours later, six hyenas were sitting around the helpless man, evidently waiting for him to pass out again. They had come close to him several times, but each time would retreat when he shouted and waved his arms. As you can imagine, we had one shaky young man on our hands.

There are exceptions with the hyena, just as there are with most other wild beasts. These exceptions have resulted in some of the most gruesome stories to come out of Africa.

The hyena is similar to a dog in appearance, but has his own peculiar shape which is not common among other members of the dog family. It appears as though the Creator played a ghastly joke on the poor fellow. His front legs are very strong, along with mighty shoulders, but his body tapers rapidly into spindly rear hips and legs. The unusually large head, with close-set ears, has strange eyes which glow with an unnatural light when seen reflected in a campfire or the headlights of a hunting car. The shape of his body causes him to move with an awkward, shambling gait, yet he has amazing agility and can get up to thirty miles an hour with little trouble. Unlike most members of the dog family, he does not trot but paces. The fore and hind feet on each side of his body move forward together like in a "pacing horse," producing a rolling gait. His feet are large and flat. When he runs down a dry riverbed at night, he sounds like a galloping horse. Yet he can be as stealthy as one of the big cats and move into a camp at night without giving himself away. He is usually betrayed by his smell, which is as high as the rotten meat he lives on. If he is upwind of camp, you can detect his presence for several hundred yards, even though he makes no sound.

It is well to keep meat hung high in a tree while in the camp area, or you are apt to wake at night to find an unwanted guest in camp. For some reason, he seems to like the presence of humans. I don't know if this is because he associates them with food, or if there is some instinct in his pea-sized brain which draws him to man. On many, many nights, I have slept with a circle of these animals sitting around camp, just outside the circle of firelight, looking for all the world like big, lopsided, shaggy dogs.

For centuries these animals have been hated and feared by the natives. As is the case with most animals who have been known to kill humans, they are associated in their pagan religion with evil spirits. It is easy to understand how the natives think of the hyena as an evil spirit in animal form, for according to a person's mood, the hyena can appear to be comical to the point of being ridiculous, or he can look like a demon incarnate. As a result of this feeling on the part of the natives, gruesome religious practices have grown up around the animals.

At one time the animals were thought to be hermaphroditic—being male one season and giving birth to young the next. The Greeks mentioned this in some of their writings. It is not true. Sexual characteristics are hard to recognize, as the male animal carries the sex organs in a sack inside his body. Lack of outward appendages has helped add to the legend.

In all my travels around Africa, I never found an individual who admitted to fondness for this animal. Still, he is a vital part of nature's plan of economy. Along with the vulture, maribou stork, and jackal, he is a very efficient garbage disposal unit, which takes care of carrion in the African brush.

Under normal conditions he prefers meat that is considerably high and on occasion, when he is not too hungry, he will drag a carcass to some secluded spot and let it rot before beginning his feast. On other occasions, he will attack live animals and even humans. When he becomes a killer, especially if he has been affected with rabies, he is a terrible thing to encounter.

Among many characteristics that do not endear him to the natives are those of waiting beside a cow which is calving and then devouring the new-born calf, or the habit of tearing the udder off a cow and devouring it.

There are documented instances of these animals attacking humans, although some men who are so-called experts on the wild animals of Africa will tell you that a hyena will not attack a human under any circumstances. I know better.

One day, a local chief sent a request for help to our station. His livestock, cattle, and camels were being decimated by packs of hyenas. Several of his herders had been badly injured by the beasts and one had been killed and dragged off. I was given the job of organizing and supervising the hunt. We moved into camp near the edge of the native village. The chief had sent one of his best men to act as guide for the hunters. He was a brother of the man who had been carried off by the animals.

After dark, the first night we were in the area, the guide's teenaged sister, along with another woman, went to the nearby water hole. This was a most unusual thing to do after dark, as this is when the great predators are on the prowl. The water hole was less than a hundred yards from our camp and we could hear the two women talking as they walked through the gathering darkness. Suddenly, both women began to scream frantically. Grabbing our rifles and flashlights, we rushed towards the water hole. In the beam of the lights, we saw a huge hyena carrying one of the girls into the brush. He was holding her in his mouth, much as a dog would carry a rabbit. We could not fire at him for fear of hitting the woman, but fired several shots into the air, hoping he would become frightened and drop the girl.

He disappeared into the brush with the hapless girl. In the thick brush which surrounded the water hole, we lost the trail and gave up the search after several fruitless hours of trying to track them. At daybreak the next morning, we set off on the trail again with several expert trackers. Our trail ended less than half a mile from the camp, when we found the bloodstained dress of the girl and some of her jewelry. The animal had completely devoured her, even to the skull.

There have been many instances of hyenas breaking into native huts. This is not hard to do, as they are flimsy affairs of mud and straw. For this reason, most individual huts and villages are surrounded by a tall, thick wall made from stout thorns, called a bomba. Even this will not stop a persistent hyena. When one breaks through, it is usually to carry off a small child, or an old person who cannot defend himself. The natives are partially to blame for the hyenas acquiring a taste for human flesh, as many tribes do not bury their dead, but leave them in the brush for the scavengers to take care of.

In some parts of East Africa, among certain of the tribes of Kenya and Tanganyika (New Tanzania), hyenas are part of their religious rites. The witches have their own hyenas which the natives say are branded with an invisible mark. These animals visit their master every night, where they are fed; sometimes the meat used is from the body of one of the witch's enemies. The cubs stay in the witch's house and he milks the females and uses the milk to make "hyena butter." Because of this, hyenas in this area are sometimes referred to as "night cattle."

While visiting near Addis Ababa, I saw an unusual ceremony revolving around witches and hyenas. An old man lived in a little mountain village, who was said to have great power over the beasts; some called him a witch, which in Africa means that he wields power over evil spirits.

After a long, tiresome trip over rough roads, we entered his hut one evening just as darkness was falling. It was a smoky, evil-smelling place. Magic symbols were hanging from the smoke-blackened walls; old, dried, human skulls, dried snakes, lizards, and what looked like a human embryo. In the center of the hut, a large iron pot was bubbling over an open fire, sending clouds of eye-watering smoke into the room. Some type of meat was cooking in the pot.

After the visitors were seated and had paid for the evening's entertainment, the old man gave directions that all were to sit quietly and not move for any reason while the hyenas were being fed. He made it quite clear, that he would not be responsible for what happened, if anyone spoke or moved while a hyena was in the hut.

The physical appearance of the witch—if that is what he was—added to the eeriness of the scene. Flickering flames from the smoky fire cast a strange light on the guests who sat cross-legged around the fire. Close in front of the bubbling pot sat the obscene figure of the hyena man.

He was old, very old. The wrinkles on his ageless face, almost hid the little eyes which glittered evilly from the deep creases. Around his neck was a necklace of human bones, mingled with the tusks of wart hogs. On his head was a band of leopard skin, with horns of a gazelle which seemed to sprout from his forehead. Mysterious bracelets of monkey fur and bird feathers were worn on wrist and ankles. Over his naked shoulders he wore the black and white cape of the Colobus monkey, the badge of authority in Africa. In his withered hand, he held a wand made from an arm bone, topped with the skull of an infant. Hunkered over the iron pot, mumbling incantations, he emanated a noticeable aura of evil and could have been an emissary of Satan himself.

As he mumbled through his ritual, he threw something into the flames which caused them to flare up with a brilliant reddish-green flame, while a foul odor permeated the hut. As the flames died, he threw back his head and from his lips came an inhuman, ululating sound which caused us all to shiver. He hesitated a few seconds with his head cocked to one side like some ancient bird; he seemed to be listening for something. Again he repeated the spine-tingling cry. Then from far in the distance came the whooping, hysterical, insane answering cry of a hyena. It was answered by others from different directions. In a little while, a ring of the foul beasts sat outside the hut.

The witch called each animal by name, while it came forward to be fed with meat from the pot, taking it carefully from the old man's hand, much like a pet dog. Forty-seven hyenas were fed that night, while an audience, captivated by fear and the unknown, sat in wondering silence. It was easy to understand how the superstitious natives lived in fear of these "so-called witches."

In some areas of Africa, witches are said to ride hyenas about the countryside in the full of the moon. This is regarded by those in the know as being very difficult and dangerous and can only be accomplished after long and arduous training. Apparently reliable eyewitnesses have given reports of seeing galloping hyenas, with a naked witch astride. They were carrying flaming torches which they refueled from time to time from a gourd of hyena butter slung over a naked shoulder.

Occasionally, a brave native will try and destroy one of these hyenas, but it is believed dangerous to do so. If the witch finds out who killed his pet, terrible retribution is visited on the hapless man and his whole family.

Among the Kikuyu tribe of Kenya for instance, old people who are no longer able to help in the economy are often left outside the bomba at night for the hyenas to devour. The same fate awaits the incurably ill. If a child is born feet first, or with a physical defect, the natives believe the

Old Gods are angry and the baby is left as a sacrifice to the hyenas. If fresh hyena dung is found outside a hut where a woman is giving birth, it the worst possible omen. The hut must be burned to the ground and the baby left for the beasts. If the first offspring is twins, the same fate awaits them.

The inherent fear of the natives for these loathsome animals was shown by an amusing incident which took place near one of our hunting camps. One evening, we came in with several wart hogs. Two of the visiting hunters had never shot a hyena, so we rigged the carcasses of the pigs for bait in the riverbed near camp. That night, one of the boys shot an unusually large hyena. We left his carcass laying in the riverbed. Early the next morning, we were wakened by a commotion from the place where we had left the animal's body. A group of boys from a nearby village had gathered around the dead animal. They were hitting it with sticks and kicking sand in its face. Finally the braver ones began to dance over the body, hitting it with a stick as they did. This gave Andy the germ for a practical joke.

That night, another hyena succumbed to our bait. Andy tied a clothesline rope around one of its legs and camouflaged the rope in the sand. One end was carried to a clump of bushes nearby. The next morning, our camp woke up early to watch the fun. When the boys arrived and began their impromptu dance over the dead hyena, Andy gave a lusty heave on the rope, which caused the hyena to rear up in a most realistic manner. The little warriors, so brave a moment before, scattered in screaming panic. When they found it was a joke, they laughed as hard as the rest of us, while some of the village men literally rolled in the sand, howling with laughter.

We learned through experience that the best way to decoy a hyena was to shoot some animal such as a gazelle, wart hog, or wildebeest, split the carcass open and then drag it behind the Land Rover, making a big circle perhaps a mile in diameter. The carcass of the bait would then be securely staked out nearby and a small amount of gasoline poured over the body and set on fire. The smell of burning flesh and hair would drift for miles on the night's air and hyenas would follow this smell like fish following a chum line. Sometimes you could hear them for hours, as they came from miles away, always being drawn closer and closer by that tantalizing smell.

Although these animals are often considered to be cowardly, when they are wounded or cornered they can be as brave and dangerous as a lion. Many times, wounded hyenas will turn on themselves and eat their own entrails and if a member of a hunting pack is wounded, it is not unusual for the rest of the animals to turn on the wounded beast and tear him to pieces.

My first experience with a wounded hyena could well have been my last. It happened during one of the first trips I took into the field. We had fixed our bait as usual; this time it was the body of an unusually large wart hog, which must have weighed well over two hundred pounds. It was roped securely to a large palm log, using a half-inch rope. About ten o'clock that night, we heard a hyena approach the camp area; he was a long way off, but was sounding like a hound dog on a hot trail. It was an hour after we first heard him that he approached the camp proper. He was a smart one. Instead of going directly to the bait, he lay under the protection of the overhanging riverbank, directly under the place where we lay in ambush. We could hear him muttering to himself in a peculiar manner hyenas have.

He was less than twenty feet away from us, but no one was about to try and scare him from his hiding place.

We waited for several hours and when we had heard nothing from him for over an hour we figured he had left. We decided to get a drink of water and go to bed. It was about two o'clock by now. As we left our positions, we heard him leave the protection of the riverbank and make a dash for the bait. Hurrying back to the edge of the river, we were in time to see him pick up the heavy carcass, snapping the rope like so much string, and slinging the body over one shoulder, make his way across the river for the opposite bank. As he leaped up the almost perpendicular bank, I fired once with my shotgun and in the dim light I thought I had hit him, even though he did not drop the pig.

This is one of the most dangerous times when you are hunting dangerous game. Hot with the thought that I had wounded the animal, I took one of the natives and crossed the river. Handing him my flashlight and telling him to stay behind me, we entered the thick brush. The trail was easy to follow, as dark red blood was splashed everywhere on the grass and leaves. I knew he was hit bad, for the color of the blood indicated arterial bleeding. I was carrying my 12 gauge over-under shotgun, loaded with two rounds of 00 buckshot.

The deeper we went into the brush, the thicker it became. Creeping "wait-a-bit" thorn bushes clutched at our clothes with such a tenacious grip I had to cut them free with my hunting knife. The rays of the full moon were blotted out in the dense underbrush. At times the brush became so thick, we had to worm forward on hands and knees. About this time, my brain began to function clearly for the first time and send danger signals to my body.

"What will happen if the beast charges you in here and

your guide drops the light and runs?" a small voice seemed to say. I had not though about this before. I had never hunted with a native and had no way of knowing how loyal he might be if the going got tough. These thoughts did little to calm my already heavily beating heart. It was not a very pleasant thought. At the time, the danger from snakes never entered my mind, yet this was the time of the night they were about and a perfect place to find them.

Just as these thoughts began to penetrate my thick skull, from a patch of heavy brush ahead came a deep, blood-curdling, chuckling growl which did little to settle my nerves.

"Fisi, M'boya sana," gasped the frightened native. "Hyena! Very bad!"

Thank God, that native was a steady man. Without waiting for my order, he shined the powerful light over my shoulder. Only a few yards away, the big hyena was crouched over the carcass of the pig. His eyes seemed to glare hatred and death at me. As the light touched him, he came for us at a shambling run which was deceptively fast. I was on both knees in the brush and fired before the stock reached my shoulder. The recoil knocked me backwards into the native, who dropped the light and we both went down in a heap. The full load of buckshot took the charging animal in the chest at lethal range and he dropped without a sound. When I finally recovered the light, I could reach out my hand and touch him.

I had to sit down a few moments and recover, for frankly I was scared and the more I thought about how stupid I had been, the more scared I became, until I lost most of the supper of guinea fowl Fadul had fed us that night.

This was one of the best lessons I learned in the brush and one that had been learned very cheaply. I never forgot it and it helped me many times later, when I was forced to go into the brush after a dangerously wounded animal. Needless to say, that native guide became one of my favorite persons and I took him with me on many hunting trips without ever regretting having done so.

Another occasion backs up my argument, "you can never tell when dealing with wild animals." A group of young soldiers on their first trip were hunting in a riverbed one night when they sighted a big hyena which had came out of some brush and was standing above them on the river-bank. One of the men fired and slightly wounded the animal. Instead of running away into the brush, as he should have, he came boiling down off the high bank in full charge at the jeep load of hunters. The only thing that kept him from joining the hunters in the jeep was one young trooper who shattered the butt of a new rifle, as he beat off the attempts of the maddened animal to get at the men.

Even after becoming Game Warden, I took time off occasionally to go hunting myself, or to take some friend into the field. I had many trophies by this time and got a real feeling of pleasure in taking a novice into the field, helping him get a good trophy and teaching him something about game conservation and the ways of wild animals. I was always fussy about the men I went hunting with. I guess this goes back to the time when I was almost shot by a drinking hunter. I had no use for the man who used a hunting trip as an excuse to get drunk and was firmly convinced that liquor had no place on a hunting trip. A cold beer in the evening after a hard day's hunt was something else, although I never touched the stuff myself.

One of my pet peeves on a hunting trip was the man who wanted to hog all the shooting for himself. One trip, I took along a sergeant major from one of the Kagnew Station units. He had been after me for a long time and had done a good deal of bragging about what a fine hunter he was. Before we had gone ten miles, I knew I had made a mistake. The gas tank of the Land Rover had been filled to the top and a bit was leaking out, causing some gas fumes in the cab. He began by fussing about the smell, then the coolness of the mountain air, finally the roughness of the road and the fact he thought I was driving around the mountain curves too fast.

Later, when we got stuck in the sand, he was full of suggestions about how to get the vehicle out, but never turned his hand to carry a rock, or an armload of palm fronds.

When we reached the campsite, he did nothing to help set up the camp and bothered one of the native boys until he stopped his work and did the job for him. That first day, I drove all day, trying to get some good trophies within range of his gun. He was never satisfied. Each time we got within range of an animal, he wanted to shoot at it and when we reached the downed animal, he was always unhappy with the size of its horns.

We came up to a herd of Grant's gazelle and before I could stop him, he stood up in the vehicle and opened fire, hitting two of the animals and only wounding them. I had warned him before hand not to shoot from the vehicle, but it had done no apparent good. When I told him we would have to trail the wounded animals, he became angry at the delay, for he had seen another buck which he thought was larger than either of the two he had shot. While we were following the wounded bucks, another animal broke from the brush about three hundred yards away and he promptly fired at him, knocking him down. When we went to examine the animal, he shrugged and said, "He's a hell of a lot smaller than I thought he was."

By this time I was in a slow boil and I told him in no un-
certain terms what I thought of him as a hunter. It did
little good, for my words seemed to bounce off like water
from a duck's back. He was such an egotist, he knew nothing he did could possibly be wrong.

He was one of the biggest blow hards I have ever met
and was a pain in the neck for all of us the whole trip. No
matter what happened, he complained. The food was lousy,
the service was lousy, and he wanted to monopolize the
conversation time too, just as he did the hunting. Needless
to say, I never invited him along on another trip, although
he asked me several times. When I got back to camp, I
made sure word about him was spread throughout the
camp and he was immediately put on the "black list." As
far as I remember, he was never taken on another hunting
trip.

One day in 1961, we planned a special trip. The party
was made up of the best hunters in Kagnew Station, not
only from the standpoint of hunting prowess, but personal-
ity wise. This trip was to be strictly for fun and to check
out a new area far to the north of Handundami, near the
Sudan border. As far as I know, no American personnel had
ever been in this area before. I knew that the bull sessions
around the campfire at night would be one of the highlights
of the entire trip.

We had run into some fantastic hunting and had picked
up some gazelle that would surely be big enough to go into
the record book. That evening, at a water hole, I knocked
over one of the largest wart hogs I had ever seen, with tusks
almost twenty inches long. I already had plans for those
tusks. They would be mounted on bases of ivory, from cross-
sections of an elephant's tusk and mounted with sterling
holders on the top. These would make a most unusual set

of candlestick holders for my sister in the States. Later she was to write:

"I sure do enjoy your gifts from Africa. This is one time when my sister-in-law can't go out and duplicate the things I get."

On our third evening in camp, we had been through an especially enjoyable bull session. We had come in from setting over some mighty ripe bait, hoping a big leopard we had seen in the vicinity might be lured by the ripe odors. After several fruitless hours, we gave up and came back to camp to sit in the warmth of the campfire, drinking the good black coffee and smoking.

It was a hot night and when I finally went to bed, I crawled into my sleeping bag in the nude, after placing my loaded shotgun within easy reach. My pistol was under the pillow as usual.

Sometime during the night, I woke with a start. There was something definitely wrong in the camp area. The evening had turned cool and I had pulled the sleeping bag over my head and I could see nothing, Still, there was something foreign in the area. For a few moments I lay like some little boy who wakes at night, disturbed by some strange sound he does not understand and who is afraid to peek out from under the covers for fear something horrible might be there ... there was a peculiar, musty odor in the air, similar to the smell which might come from an opened grave. I couldn't identify it at the time.

Suddenly a twig snapped nearby and I sat upright, reaching instinctively for my pistol and the flashlight. There, less than five feet away, sat the biggest, meanest-looking hyena I had even seen. He was sitting like some big dog and I knew what Ellie had meant when she said: "He was licking his chops."

I'm not exactly sure what happened next, but suddenly I found myself standing naked in the center of the camp, shotgun in one hand and flashlight in the other. For some reason I had put on my safari hat, although I had on no slippers and the ground was covered with murderous acacia thorns.

As I moved, the hyena turned to run, looking back over his shoulder and as a result ran full tilt into the kitchen area, upsetting the pots and pans with a terrific clatter and scaring the devil out of the native boys who were sleeping nearby. When he hit the pans, he yelped, much like some domestic dog which has been hit with a stick.

At the edge of the camp area, he stopped for a moment to look at me and it was then that I fired. If you want some excitement, try firing a 12 gauge shotgun with one hand, while you try and focus a large flashlight with the other, especially when you are trying to balance on one naked foot in the middle of a pile of thorns. It was quite evident from the results that the butt of the gun was not held solid against my shoulder. I must have had my fingers on both triggers, for both barrels went off with a mighty blast, knocking me flat on the thorns, on my naked hide.

As if by a pre-arranged signal, every light in camp was turned on, focused on the "great white hunter," laying naked on his back, blinking foolishly, with shotgun in hand. For months afterward, I would be approached by wives of these hunters in the commissary, or the club. Their inevitable question:

"Jack, what is the well-dressed hyena hunter wearing these days?"

I never quite lived this down and the incident was blown up all out of proportion, until it became one of those stories told to newcomers. I might go further and say there were many added embellishments which were far from being true.

One day, just wandering around in the brush, we found a young hyena pup and decided to capture it. The little fellow was possibly two months old, but already he had a mind of his own. One of the native boys approached him from the front, while I tried to capture him with a net made from an old mosquito netting. The pup was far from scared of us. He was quite belligerent. As we approached, he snarled fiercely and gave weird little cries I am sure were meant to frighten us. When Cookie was about eight feet from him, the little fellow made a dash at the camp boy, catching hold of his trouser leg. We howled with laughter, as Cookie tried to kick loose. The pup held on like a bulldog, shaking his head and growling all the while. I finally calmed down enough to go to Cookie's rescue, but when I pried him off the frightened boy, I had my hands full with a snarling, biting little demon. Finally he quieted down and I put him in a cage made from branches and vines.

Within a few days he was as tame as any domestic puppy. The only trouble was that he didn't know his own strength. When we would sit around the camp fire, he loved to come up and worry our shoes, but when the tustle became a bit violent, he would bite through the shoe. This resulted in some sore feet, some unkind remarks about hyenas in general, and a few swats on the little fellow's rear end.

When we got back to Kagnew Station, we found he loved to take a shower, biting at the stream of water and making weird sounds such as only a hyena can make. The children loved to come and watch him and would tease him into laughing at them.

For some reason he didn't like women and this was his undoing. One day, when he was about six months old—he already weighed close to seventy-five pounds—I had him out for a walk. He was on a leash. A major's wife walked by and before I realized what was happening, the little imp jerked free and treed the officer's wife on a pile of lumber nearby. Neither the major nor his wife had a very good sense of humor and we were ordered to get rid of our pet. We thought it was hilarious and the colonel admitted to me later, it was one of the funniest stories he had ever heard. Abdullah, as we called him, was the only hyena I ever really liked.

Although I didn't have a deep regard for these animals, I got used to having them around. They were as much a part of the African scene as the palm trees, the water holes, the lovely sunsets, and the flocks of sand grouse. They also made for a sweeter-smelling camp area. They had their place in the scheme of things and I didn't mind them as long as they stayed out of my bedroom.

6 Snakes Ain't for Cushions

Most hunters going into the African bush for the first time fear snakes more than any other single thing. This is not unusual, for most humans detest snakes. It is a universal fear which goes back to the beginning of time.

To deny this danger would be similar to denying the danger in driving on the Los Angeles Freeway. With the possible exception of India and the area once known as Indo China, Africa leads the world in snake population. However, this does little to deter the dedicated sportsman. The appalling rate of deaths on our public highways does little to keep the traveler at home. Danger increases as you go looking for it. The teenager who plays "chicken" behind the wheel of a high-powered car is more apt to become a statistic than one who obeys the law. This is true of the big game hunter, whether he is tyro or professional.

On occasions I walked close to dangerous animals in Africa, while trying to photograph them. I used extreme caution and did nothing to arouse their belligerent instincts. As a result they presented no problem. From careful observation of hundreds of wild things all over the world, I have come to this conclusion. Most animals, or reptiles which could be dangerous, will not molest a human unless they have been cornered, wounded, persistently annoyed, or are protecting their young.

I have walked within ten feet of a huge brown bear fishing for salmon on the Kodiak Peninsula of Alaska. All the notice he gave was to look in my direction and give me a dirty look which was warning enough. Yet a friend of mine was chased up a tree in the suburbs of Anchorage, when he made the mistake of getting between a cow moose and her month old calf. The same rule never applies twice when dealing with dangerous wild animals. There are even a few relatively harmless and gentle animals in Africa who will become quite fierce if their young are molested.

One of the cardinal rules for approaching any dangerous animal on foot is to move slowly and cautiously. Stop when the animal appears to become restless or annoyed. Keep downwind of him wherever possible. Sometimes when you are stalking an animal in heavy cover, the wind will shift playing tricks on you which can prove disastrous. There are times when a wild animal will allow a human to come within touching distance of him. He may see you and still not become nervous. But let him get one whiff of man odor and he will probably run or charge, depending on his disposition. Another rule to remember is this. Never make a sudden move, or run, if you are close to dangerous game. This will often trigger a charge and is especially true of cape buffalo or rhinoceros.

This same reasoning can be applied when dealing with snakes. Given half a chance, most snakes will try and get out of your way, although there are a few varieties in Africa which will attack, sometimes on sight.

The African puff adder, sometimes called the "death adder," is one of the ugliest and deadliest of the snake family. He accounts for most of the snake-bite deaths in Africa. A relative of our rattlesnake, he is usually sluggish. Arouse him and he will dispute the passage of man or beast. This repulsive fellow is usually found in the desert, or in sandy areas of the veldt. He lies camouflaged in the sand, until someone steps on or near him. His strike, especially against a barefooted native, usually means death within a few minutes.

Snakes are as much a part of the African scene as the insects that are present at all times, and are usually much less of a problem. Most times you will not see them, for most of them are nocturnal and do most of their hunting at night. Many of them would die if they were exposed to the hot, noonday sun. During twenty-eight safari trips into the hinterlands of Ethiopia and Sudan, I saw a total of seven snakes, all but one of these were poisonous.

The sinister beauty of the cobra has always fascinated me. In areas where we hunted regularly, there were two varieties of this snake: the common Egyptian cobra, which reaches a length of eight feet, and his vicious relative the "black necked" or "spitting cobra." The Egyptian cobra favors dry regions and will often be found around the edges of desert areas. It's hood is less spectacular than that of the Indian cobra. Both of these snakes have the habit of standing on their tails, swaying from side to side when they are in the position to attack. Both are aggressive and will attack with little provocation. The "spitting cobra" seldom reaches a length of seven feet, but makes up in size by its ability to eject venom. It will spit a stream of the yellow-colored poison in rapid succession, sometimes as many as fifteen times and up to a distance of ten feet. In

Ethiopia this snake is usually a brick-red color with a black band behind the throat. Both of these cobras are extremely venomous and death will occur rapidly unless immediate first aid is given, including the injection of proper snake bite anti-venom.

The venom from the spitting cobra will not kill on contact, but if it gets into the eyes will cause temporary blindness and great pain. This is the target the snake usually aims for.

During the spring of 1960, an American soldier hunting on the desolate plains of the Dongali Desert in southeastern Eritrea tangled with one of this breed and was struck in the face by squirted venom.

"The pain was so great," he told me later, " it was as if someone had thrown acid in my eyes."

With great presence of mind, his native guide urinated in his eyes, washing the poison out and possibly saving the man's eyesight. It was several weeks before he fully recovered.

In many miles covered in the bush, I only saw one cobra. Driving along an obscure trail in high grass one day, I was startled when a big cobra reared out of the grass beside the trail. I knew if I drove past the snake, it would be in a perfect position to strike at my passenger, so without thinking I turned the wheel and drove over the snake. Thinking I had killed it and knowing its hide would make a beautiful trophy, I stopped to collect it. It was nowhere to be found. I often wondered later what we would have done if the snake had come out from under the car and attacked us in the tall grass.

Probably the most feared snake in Africa is the mamba, or "tree cobra." There are five varieties of this snake on the continent south of the Sahara and none of them resembles other cobras. They are a long, slender snake, somewhat resembling the "blue racer" of our Midwest states. A snake ten feet long will be as big around as a man's thumb. They move with amazing agility, with the front third of their body reared off the ground. Experts say they can outrun a fast horse.

Many times mambas travel in pairs, male and female, so if you kill one, it is well to be on the lookout for the other close by.

Mambas have the worst disposition of any snake in Africa and will often attack without provocation. Usually they will be found in bushes, or lying on rocks, where they will strike at the face of anyone who passes close by. Their bite is usually fatal.

My first encounter with a mamba came during my second season as a Game Warden. I was visiting a hunting camp on the Baraka River, some seventy miles northwest of the village of Hadundami. The hunters had run into some exceptional wart-hog trophies and I went out with them one morning and shot a big boar whose tusks measured over eighteen inches long.

They had a young fellow with them, on his first hunting trip. It didn't take long to find that he was a city boy and had never slept out in the wilderness before. It seemed as though his fears centered on snakes and hyenas, so they let him sleep in the back of one of the trucks.

I had been invited to set up camp nearby and enjoy the evening meal with them. Dinner was a delicious suckling pig which had been cooked over the open fire. As we sat around smoking and talking after dinner, the neophyte asked, in a rather embarrassed manner, the location of bathroom facilities. One of the hunters looked up from where he was whetting a hunting knife and in a rather sarcastic manner said:

"There's a wooden seat out behind those bushes," pointing, "but you better take along a flashlight, as there is apt to be a hyena around somewhere. Be careful to check the ground too. The last trip we were on, a fellow got bit on the fanny by a snake and we had a hell of a time trying to put on a tourniquet." Everyone thought this was funny except the newcomer.

The next morning, I left early to check with another party nearby and came back about eleven o'clock, just as it was beginning to get hot. One of the boys had come in with a beautiful, record book Sommering gazelle.

As it was time for siesta, I set up my cot in the shade of a big tree. While lying there, one of the men called to me:

"Come here a minute Jack, I want to show you something strange."

I got up and went over to his cot, which was set up under a low hanging limb covered with a green, fibrous vine.

"Look up there," he said quietly, pointing to a limb overhead. Do you see that little bird that looks like a canary?"

I saw a small bird in the branches overhead; it was throwing a fit, screaming and beating its wings frantically. As we watched it closely, the bird slowly began to disappear. Suddenly there was no more bird, We checked closely and found a long, slender, green snake lying on a limb over the cot. There was a suspicious bulge in its body just back of the head. Picking up his shotgun, he blew the snake from the limb. At the sound of the shot, the camp boys came running. When they saw the long, green snake lying on the ground, they were petrified, saying over and over again:

"M'boya sana! M'boya sana!" "Very bad! Very bad!"

When the boys had calmed down a bit, we found out it was a green mamba.

"You should watch for the other now," they said, "it will be looking to do you harm."

Later that afternoon, I went out into the underbrush near camp, following one of the native guides on a pig trail. I stumbled over a protruding root and threw out my hand to keep from falling. As I did something swished past my face and struck a heavy blow on the shoulder of my thick hunting jacket. I heard the guide yell and looked up just in time to see him decapitate another of the green snakes with his heavy brush knife. The mamba had evidently been lying on a branch and had struck at my face as I passed. When I stumbled, it missed its target by inches.

This was the snakiest trip I was ever on and we had one more episode with our scaly friends before it was over. This one was not only excruciatingly funny to the bystanders, but it probably ruined the hunting career of our newcomer and almost made a mental case out of him.

The morning of the third day in camp, we wakened to the screaming of a herd of baboons. They sounded so loud I was sure they must be in the camp area. Peeking out of my sleeping bag I confirmed this. They were not only in the camp area, they were all over it. One old male was sitting solemnly in a folding chair near my cot, looking me over and emitting short barks as though to say:

"What in world have we here?"

Our greenhorn hunter awoke at the noise and looked out to find his truck covered with baboons. Two of them were hanging over the rear of the truck, eyeing him with suspicion. He reacted in typical fashion and we sat back to watch the fun.

He came boiling out of the truck in his underwear, shotgun in hand. The baboons scattered into the trees, and began to insult him in the most approved baboon fashion. There is no animal who can become so insulting as a baboon. They leap into the air, turn handsprings, and throw anything handy, acting for all the world like some little boys who are trying to start a fight.

"I'll get those damned monkeys," Joe screamed, shaking his fist in the direction of the apes. "No blankety blank baboon is going to make an ass out of me."

We didn't tell him then, but that was just what they were doing.

Every time Joe would place the gun to his shoulder to fire, they would move out of range. He was getting pretty angry and using some mighty bad language. We sat back and howled, which made it all the worse. He determined to prove he was a good hunter. Following the herd out on the plain, he chased them towards a little hill which was about five hundred yards from camp. As the apes moved towards the hill, Joe decided to outsmart them. The apes went around the left of the hill and Joe went to the right.

There were many deep gullies coming down off the hill and we were not surprised when Joe disappeared into one of them. However, we were not prepared for the blood-curdling scream of fear and horror which came from the gully immediately afterwards. Dashing for our guns, we piled into the nearest jeep and rushed to his rescue. There was no one in the gully. His shotgun lay beside the prints made where his boots had landed in the sand. We began to look around and soon saw him climb over the lip of the gully about a hundred yards away. When we reached him, he was trembling as if he had a chill. His face was the color of putty.

"What in the world happened to you?" I asked.

"I don't know," he gasped, when he could get back his breath. "When I jumped off that bank, I landed on top of the biggest damned snake I've ever seen. I was so scared I dropped my gun and ran. As I looked back, there he was right behind me."

We returned to the spot where he had jumped into the gully. Beside the prints of his boots was the unmistakeable track of a big snake. The python had evidently been sunning himself on the sand, when Joe came hurtling down from above. I don't really believe the snake chased Joe. I think he was scared too and just happened to run in the same direction. We found the place where it entered the brush. There was no question that it was a "granddaddy" in size, for the track it made was a good eighteen inches wide.

Joe was ruined for any more country life and stayed in camp until that hunt was over. As far as I can remember, he never went out on another hunt.

This episode brings up the question. Are these big snakes dangerous to man? Some stories would lead you to believe they will attack humans. While doing some investigation on my own I ran into some pretty fantastic stories concerning these big snakes, but I never found anyone who could authenticate a story of one attacking a human.

There is no question that one of these big fellows could be a mighty rough customer if aroused and it is quite obvious that under the right conditions one could overpower a man.

A python will kill and eat a good-sized animal. I saw one which had killed and eaten a large pig, while another time I came across one which had devoured a gazelle the size of a white-tailed deer. The bones of the animal had been crushed in the constricting coils and it had been swallowed whole. The snake was dead, for the gazelles horns had pierced through its sides.

Many times I made temporary headquarters in the rest hotel at Cheren, for it was sixty miles closer to the hunting area than Asmara and saved a good deal of hard travel. One day, two natives came to the hotel with word they had located a big snake in the mountains north of town. "Would I like to help them catch it?" they asked.

I was delighted. We went on foot up a rocky ravine, to where the python had his lair, moving carefully in the rocks so as not to disturb the big snake, keeping a careful watch out for smaller and deadlier members of the snake family.

As the day began to warm, the big snake came out of a hole in the rocks. First the big head appeared, almost a foot long and six inches wide. This inched out of the hole to be followed by coil after coil of a body which was at least a foot thick. When I saw the size of this big fellow, it was easy to believe a story I had heard a few days before. On this same mountain, the natives had come on a dead snake, with a full grown leopard in its coils. That must have been a "battle royal."

The snake's body was a beautiful gray-green, with lovely markings which blended in perfectly with the surroundings. When he was in the open, I shot it in the head with my shotgun. Before I could stop them, the two natives were on the writhing snake, spearing it over and over again. I have the skin now, full of spear holes, on the wall of my den. It is over eighteen feet long.

Most of the natives living in the lowlands of Ethiopia and Sudan wear snake charms which are supposed to protect them from snake bite. These charms are made from tanned pieces of camel's hide, which have been sewn to form little pouches about an inch square and half an inch thick. An intricate design is punched in the leather. Inside each pouch is a pinch of dried cobra venom and other ingredients known only to the witch doctor who prepares the charm. After proper ceremonies, the pouches are attached to a braided band of camel's hide and are worn on the left arm over the biceps.

Scorpions and millipeds are much more of a problem in the hunting areas than snakes. The bite of a milliped or "thousand legged" worm, while painful, is not dangerous. The bite of the common scorpion—sting is a better word to use—will cause a man to have nausea, fainting spells, and pain so bad he wishes he were dead. There is also a type of scorpion found in the lowlands during the rainy seasons which grows to a length of ten inches and is supposed to be fatal.

One of the first lessons to learn in the hunting camp is to shake out clothing and shoes before putting them on in the morning, for these are favorite places for scorpions to hide. Sometimes you will see them moving around the camp area, with their tails cocked over their back. They will sting you in a flash if you get close enough. Surprisingly enough, the best remedy for a scorpion bite is that used by our Indians of the Southwest plains—a common mud pack.

On my last trip to Sudan in 1962, we camped under a huge tree which must have been thirty feet in diameter. Its shade covered at least half an acre and its huge, protruding roots made excellent benches in the camp area. During the eighteen days we worked out of this camp, we never saw a scorpion or snake in the area. Several months later, another camping party, using the same place, was caught in a freak rain storm that drenched the area. The next morning, they killed twelve mamba and over two hundred scorpions. Evidently they had been hiding under the roots of the tree.

Cobras are kept pretty much under control by snake hunters who kill the reptiles for their hides which make beautiful purses and shoes. For some reason, this is one creature the conservationists do not worry about.

In spite of all I've written in this chapter, don't let snakes keep you from visiting Africa. Chances are, you will never see one.

7 Here Kitty! Kitty! Kitty!

If you were to take a vote as to which is the most popular of all wild animals, I believe the lion would win hands down. This popularity can be easily proven at any zoo. People will crowd around the monkey cages to watch their antics. Others will prefer the clowning of the bears or the trained seals. But let a lion roar just once and most of these folks will rush over to see what the "king of the beasts" is doing.

Man has dubbed this magnificent animal the "king." Actually he doesn't qualify for this title in the wild animal kingdom. The elephant is more powerful and probably more intelligent. The cape buffalo is more vicious and the leopard faster. Still, there is something regal about this animal which places him in a special class of his own.

While visiting in Uganda, a professional hunter, speaking with that special dry humor the British seem to possess, told me this story about the king:

It seems as though a particular lion wasn't getting the attention he craved, so he went on a rampage through the jungle. Coming up to a baboon, he roared:

"Who is king of the beasts?"

"You are sire," said the monkey trembling with fear.

A little farther on, he came to a zebra grazing on some lilies:

"Who is king of the beasts?" the lion roared again.

"You are sire," said the frightened zebra.

This went on for some time, until the lion's wounded ego began to be restored. Finally he came to where an old elephant was belly deep in some water, feeding on water tender grass.

"Who is king of the beasts?" the lion roared again.

The old elephant didn't answer, in fact he didn't even look up from where he was feeding. He just reached out, grabbed the lion around the body with his trunk and slammed him against the trunk of a tree nearby and went on with his feeding.

The lion lay stunned for a few moments, then staggered to his feet and went off muttering under his breath:

"Some folks just don't have a sense of humor."

We often think of animals in terms of human attributes. I once had a beautiful Irish Setter by the name of Prince Eric Red. The Prince thought he was human. At least he acted that way. I have seen cats, especially Persians, who were as stuck up as any human could possibly be. Looking back through my own life, I can catalogue a lot of people who possessed animal characteristics. There is the human pig. There are those who possess the worst traits of the hyena and even a few who resemble vultures. It is not hard to see the similarity between man and lion.

In general the lion is similar to man, in that he kills for food rather than pleasure. There are a few of each species who are true killers and these are the ones who make trouble both in the animal kingdom and in human society.

The lion resembles man in his insatiable curiosity. This is especially true of the lioness, just as it is among the female of the human species. I have observed lions closely, both on protected game preserves and in the wilds. The "wild" lion seems to be more curious than the one who sees humans almost everyday.

Once while riding through some heavy brush in southern Sudan, I had to stop the Land Rover to keep from running over the tail of a lioness. She was laying in some grass, watching a herd of gazelle grazing nearby. She never even bothered to look in our direction. After about ten minutes, she stood up, yawned in our faces, showing the pink cavern of her throat and her enormous canines. Then she approached the vehicle, sniffed at the front tire, and retreated into the brush without having once lost her composure.

Another similarity between man and lion is that they both walk the earth as though they owned it. They seem to think everything has been placed here just for their own personal use.

Many stories have been woven around "simba," as he is called in the Swahili language. For years, he was pictured as a ferocious man-killer, who had to be wiped off the face of the earth.

In most cases, you will find the lion is a gentleman, who will do almost anything to keep his dignity. Given a chance, ninety-nine times out of a hundred he will retreat gracefully. Don't back him into a corner or what he thinks is a corner, or you are apt to be in for trouble. Don't ever do anything to make him lose his dignity, or to make him look silly, or you are apt to have an angry lion on your hands and an angry lion is nothing but trouble.

There have been man-eating lions in African history and there will no doubt be more of them. The most famous of these were probably the man-eaters of Tsavo. They halted the buildings of the Mombasa-Nairobi Railroad in 1899. So many of the native workers were being dragged off into the brush and eaten, they had to halt work until professional hunters could be called in to kill the beasts. Some authorities blamed the natives as much as the lions. They said that when a native died, instead of burying him, his friends would often drag the body into the brush and leave it. Undoubtedly these bodies were eaten by lions, who developed a liking for human flesh. It has been pretty well proven that when a lion has eaten human flesh one time, he will be back for more. This is especially true when he finds out how easy it is to catch and kill a human.

When I visited Tanganyika in 1959, a native postman was dragged off his bicycle in the outskirts of Dar Es Salaam and devoured by a lion. Usually a lion becomes a man killer when he gets too old to kill other game, or when he has been crippled from a wound. This is one of the reasons why hunting laws are so strict in this part of the country. If a professional hunter allows his client to wound a dangerous animal and let it escape into the brush, he is required by law to track it down and destroy it, as it may become dangerous to the first human it meets. He is liable to lose his guide's license and get a heavy fine if he fails to do this. Your chances of meeting a man-killing lion, or rather I should say a man-eating lion in the African bush, is less than that of meeting a murderer on the streets of one of our large cities.

Generally speaking, when a lion is not hungry, he is pretty good natured. The family group, called a "pride," will play together like a family of domestic cats, licking each other's faces and showing every indication of affection. Mothers and cubs will often be seen playing together. It is amusing to watch the cubs climb over their's mother's back, pulling her whiskers and sometimes chomping on her tail. If they get a bit too rough, she will cuff them without mercy.

It is not unusual to see a large male lie in the shade of a bush when he has eaten his fill, while the very animals he usually feeds on play within easy reach. I have seen Thompson gazelle walk up under the nose of a lion and flick their tails in his face, without getting the slightest reaction from him. It is as though they know the king has eaten and is content. If he is hungry, there will be no other animal in sight.

The lioness does much of the hunting for the family, while papa does the more dignified work of scaring the prey. The lioness will drift downwind, quiet as a shadow, until she lies in the grass hidden from a herd of gazelle, zebra, or topi. The male will go upwind until his scent drifts to the grazing animals. Once the animals scent papa, they become frantic and begin to run every way to escape. To increase their panic, the male roars, holding his head close to the ground, so that the terrifying sound rolls along the ground. Usually one of the panic-stricken animals will come within range of the waiting lioness.

In attacking zebra, an experienced hunter will sometimes gallop alongside the straining animal and slap it on the neck with its paw, then slow down and wait for the animal to fall. The blow may not even break the skin, but will dislocate the animal's neck. Most often, the lioness will sink her teeth into the neck of the prey. With one paw hooked into the shoulder of the victim, she will reach around the animal's neck with the other, grasping the beast by its nose and twisting its head back until the neck breaks.

Often after a kill, the male will drive the female and cubs away until he has eaten his fill. He does not seem to mind other males eating with him and sometimes there will be as many as six males eating peacefully off one carcass.

When the lord and master finishes his feeding, the lioness and cubs will come and eat. It is amusing to watch the small cubs learning to eat meat. They will fight among themselves over some choice tidbit, even though there is plenty for all. Snarling and "pff-tting" like angry cats, they will often fight until mamma becomes angry and smacks them away from the carcass so she can eat in peace.

The king usually gets along with smaller scavengers and will often allow a jackal to feed with him. He hates hyenas and vultures and will do anything to keep them away from his kill, even when he has finished eating. It is not unusual to see a lion wake from his sleep and come charging out from the shade of a bush to drive away the ever-present vultures. One day, I saw a big male standing on the carcass of a wildebeest swatting at the vultures as they swooped low overhead.

Big, beautiful, and loveable as he may look with a full belly, he is "muy malo" (very bad) when he gets angry. In this too he resembles a human. He hates pain worse than anything else. If he has a toothache, or has porcupine quills in a foot pad, or maybe has just a plain bellyache, his mood will change from that of a big, lovable pussy cat, to one of the most ferocious animals imaginable. Sometimes when this happens, his disposition becomes so bad his family drives him out and he becomes an outcast. It is usually during times like these that he becomes a man-eater.

During the breeding season, the lion becomes vicious and unpredictable and will often turn on its own kind. Sometimes a male must defeat three or four rivals in bloody combat to claim the favors of a lioness.

After the battle is won, the victor will go off with his

"lady love" until they find a place of suitable privacy. During the next two weeks, it is extremely dangerous to approach their hideout, for they will attack man or beast. This is not the usual characteristic of these animals, for I have taken many pictures of prides of lion, from fifty feet or less, with no sign of ill will being shown.

About 108 days after mating, a litter of four and sometimes as many as six cubs will be born. The new babies are usually about the size of housecats. The cubs will be nursed for three months and will not kill for themselves until they are a year old. A lion will reach his prime at five or six years and may live for twenty-five years, with fifteen being a fair average.

There is nothing more awe inspiring in the animal kingdom than an angry, wounded lion. Even the fierce anger of the elephant or cape buffalo will not reach the same peak as that of the lion. Crouching low in the grass, his eyes will literally seem to shoot sparks. His mane will stand on end and his tail will be as stiff as a poker. It will begin to jerk from side to side as he prepares to charge. All the while, a deep, rumbling roar will be coming from deep in his throat, which does a lot to lower the morale of the best hunter.

Under pain, which naturally infuriates him, huge amounts of adrenalin are shot into his blood stream. When he finally moves, it will be like a projectile shot from a cannon. He will appear as a tawny streak skimming over the ground, eating up twenty-five feet at a leap. At this rate, he covers a hundred yards in four seconds. This means the hunter is very lucky to get in a second aimed shot, if he misses with the first. This is one of the reasons so many professional hunters prefer the double barrel express rifle. (They can get off the second shot much faster than with a bolt action

Tiang—a horse antelope—shot in the Sudan in 1962.

Jack Mohr shown here with camp boy Cookie looking over record major kudu shot in Eritrea in 1959. The horns measure 58½ inches.

Author Jack Mohr with a rare roan antelope.

Ethiopian patriarchs heading into Axsum.

Ethiopian mountain village.

The mysterious obelisk of Axsum.

Typical Eritrea kudu country.

Boss Grythe and author Jack Mohr's son Dwight.

rifle.) All the while he is in his charge, he will be giving off blood-curdling sounds which tell you just exactly what will happen when he gets hold of you.

Under normal circumstances a lion is not difficult to kill. He is a thin-skinned animal with a delicate nervous system that reacts quickly to shock. If you knock him off his feet, keep him down! A lion which is downed and then allowed to get to his feet again is the lion which will cause you trouble. Once he gets moving a second time—and this will be within a split second—he can carry an awful lot of lead and still live to kill the hunter. This is why one of the cardinal rules of big game hunting is to get close enough so your first shot will place the quarry on the ground. Then keep him down! Once the lion is dead, or you think he is dead, approach with caution. It is always wise, when dealing with dangerous game, to smack him with an extra shot even though you're sure he is dead. I've seen some dead animals get up off the ground and cause considerable panic.

My only lion trophy was a fine male shot in southern Sudan. Stalking a pride of four males, I was able to get within thirty-five yards of them as they lay in the shade of a thorn tree. When the biggest one stood up, I busted him in the off shoulder with a soft-nosed, 250 grain bullet from my .338 magnum. The shock of the striking bullet flipped him end for end. He never got up, but just to make sure, I busted him again before I approached. The first shot had broken both shoulders and killed him instantly. This shoulder shot is the best to use on dangerous game. With a heart or lung shot, animals will often travel several hundred yards—sometimes more—before dying.

The lion is a master of camouflage and can hide his four-hundred-pound bulk in a patch of grass that you would swear could not conceal a jackrabbit. Unlike many wild animals, he is not afraid of lights at night. He will often come into the cone of light made by the headlights of a vehicle. Once while driving across the veldt after dark, I saw a pride of five lions standing near some brush. I stopped the Rover to see what they would do. One of the big males and a lioness walked over to investigate. The male spent several minutes scratching his back on the front fender, while purring like a gigantic tea kettle.

In many areas of Africa, from central Sudan to the southern plains of Tanganyika, the plains teem with herds of wild life: antelope, gazelle, zebra, and others. Usually where you find these animals, you will find the big cats. The smaller gazelle are favorites of the cheetah. The beautiful leopard will eat anything, even hyena, while the lion prefers zebra and the larger of the gazelle.

During the early occupation of Eritrea, most of the lion population was killed off by professional hunters. There are still many leopards and cheetah in this area and both are protected by law.

The leopard far outstrips both the lion and tiger in pure malevolence and basic savagery. Although smaller than both, its fighting ability is barely inferior. Most African natives fear the leopard far more than the larger and stronger lion.

In intelligence, the leopard ranks high. It learns quickly and retains anything that is to its advantage. It will often use wily tactics to capture its prey. Gazelles are notorious for their curiosity and a leopard will sometimes roll in the grass until the curious gazelle comes within range.

The domestic dog is one of the leopard's favorite and as a result they will sometimes come into a village and even enter a house to steal a dog. When a leopard becomes a man-killer, he will sometimes kill large numbers of people in a short time.

The lion always eats what he kills, or will leave some for the scavengers. The leopard on the other hand kills for the sheer savage fun of it and will often leave its prey and go off in search of another victim.

There is no doubt that the spotted cat is beautiful; he is also vicious, bloodthirsty, and the most unpredictable of all wild animals. Professional hunters place him high on the list of most dangerous animals; some place him on top.

Leopard hunting offers a real challenge to even the most dedicated hunter, as they are among the most difficult of all animals to hunt. Take into consideration their extreme caution and their vicious nature. Add speed, exceptional sense of smell, sight, and hearing. Add again a generous measure of devilish intelligence and you have an animal which will match wits with the finest hunter. Quite often the leopard hunter will find the tables turned and that he has become the hunted instead of being the hunter.

On my last Sudan trip, we baited a tree for leopard, using the carcass of a topi. Night after fruitless night we sat in that blind for hours on end, remaining absolutely quiet and motionless. We could not even slap at the pesky mosquitoes which resisted the merits of our anti-mosquito juice. Early every morning, we went back to camp completely frustrated. We could see signs that the leopard had been in the close neighborhood and one night he even came and ate part of the bait before our very eyes without warning us. We never even had a glimpse of him.

On the sixth night, I about had it and decided to do some other type of hunting for a spell. Local natives told me that some exceptional pigs were to be found in the corn fields which bordered the river. The fields were close to camp and I didn't bother to take a guide with me. Armed with my shotgun and with an electric hunting light attached to my cap, I ventured into the fields. I was no more than fifty yards inside the first field when I heard a slight rustling from up ahead. Snapping the safety off my gun and turning on the light, I was startled. There less than fifty feet away were two of the most beautiful leopards I had ever seen. Without thinking I threw the gun to my shoulder and fired twice in rapid succession. Both cats dropped, twitched a few times, and lay still. I had sense enough to reload before approaching them.

It wasn't until later, when I had time to think, that I realized what a foolish thing I had done. The female lay with five 00 buckshot pellets in her, but the big male, who was almost nine feet long, had a single pellet in his head. As I went over the action in retrospect, I wondered what would have happened if the male had been merely wounded instead of being killed with the first shot. With my gun unloaded, I would never have had time to reload before the wounded leopard would have been on me. I would probably have become another of those statistics available in Africa, which show how foolish some humans can be. How I got so close to the cats, I'll never know.

In southern Ethiopia, there are a few of the lovely jet black leopards, sometimes called "black panthers." They have a golden tinge of rosettes which show through the jet black of their coats and have the reputation of being the most vicious of an already vicious family.

One of Africa's animals which has never failed to interest me is the cheetah. This beast is probably best known for the fact that since time immemorial, it has been used as a hunting cat by royalty. The average cheetah has a lovely disposition, will tame easily, becomes genuinely affectionate and will follow his master around like a dog. He is the most graceful of the cat family, I believe, and surely the fastest of all four-footed animals. His speed over short distances is phenomenal. He moves so fast, that he appears as a yellowish blur, floating over the ground. He can overtake the fleetest gazelle without appearing to exert himself. From a sitting position, he can reach a speed of 45 miles per hour in two seconds and has been clocked at over seventy miles per hour. His stamina at this speed is short and he can only run all out for a distance of possibly five hundred yards.

The cheetah, while very beautiful, is also strange looking, for he has the head of a dog, on a cat's body. His claws are blunt, not like the scythes of the leopard and they are not retractable, so he leaves tracks like a dog.

An Italian friend of mine in Asmara had one for a pet. The big cat loved to have his stomach scratched and he would lay on his back with all four feet waving in the air and purr like a deep-noted teakettle when you indulged him.

I never had much desire to shoot any of the big cats, with the exception of the leopard, which I hated almost as much as the hyena. I admired the lion too much to want to shoot him and the cheetah seemed almost like a house pet.

There were times, I realized, when the lion had become a dangerous nuisance and had to be killed. When the Italians first came to Eritrea in the late 1890's, the big cats were dangerous. As a result, professional lion hunters came into their own. I met one of these old timers, an ex-Italian nobleman who lived on the outskirts of Agordat. He killed over 150 lions during a period that lasted from 1920 until he shot the last of his big cats in 1946.

He had a unique method of killing the big cats and used a shotgun exclusively. His body was covered with claw scars. An old Englishman living in Massawa told of going on a hunt with the Italian in 1932:

"We walked close to a big pride of lions which were in

the shade of an acacia tree," he said. "Antonio had me throw rocks at them until a big male became angry and charged. I thought Antonio had gone crazy, for he stood as still as a statue while the hurtling lion came rapidly closer. 'Shoot! Shoot!' I screamed, "but he never moved until the lion had left the ground in his last leap from less than thirty feet away. When the big beast was in the middle of his leap, Antonio calmly raised his gun and shot. He had to step to one side so the beast could fall to the ground at our feet. I could reach out with my hand and touch the still quivering body. One hunting trip with the count was enough for me."

The count was one of a vanishing breed, that frankly I'm glad is dying out. These are the men who kill for profit and for the pleasure of killing, such men as the buffalo hunters who depopulated our western plains and left them piled high with the dry bones of animals they had killed.

Today, with sensible hunting laws and stiffer game enforcement, the big cats are coming back. A few years ago in southern Ethiopia, the leopard was hunted almost to extinction when the vogue for ladies' leopard skin coats reached its peak. Now you need a special permit to hunt them and they are on the increase.

8 Thick-hided Customers

Shortly after arriving in Eritrea, I moved into a house in the city of Asmara. My neighbor was a Norwegian gentleman, who was to become my best friend. Bosse Grythe came to Ethiopia in 1950 to work with the State Bank of Ethiopia. He was the Foreign Exchange Controller when I met him. One day, working in my yard, I saw this little man working next door and asked him if he spoke English.

"Ya a little," he said.

I invited him in for a cup of coffee, never realizing this was to be the beginning of a very close friendship which lasts until this day.

Bosse is one of those human rarities you meet once in a lifetime. He refuses to believe anything bad about anyone, unless maybe it is the Communists who are his "pet peeve." Because of this inclination and the fact he is a natural humorist, I have never known anyone who is more fun to be around. Every moment of every day is a new experience for Bosse. Even when he is feeling "under the weather," he greets each new experience in life with a hearty "faan'tas-tic!" He is a little man by physical standards, standing about

135

five foot seven inches tall, but he is a giant in every other way.

Aud, his wife, is one of the most beautiful redheaded Amazons I have ever met and is every bit as fine a person as her husband. They make a rare couple. This was for me one of those "once-in-a-lifetime" friendships.

Whenever Bosse could tear himself away from his bank job, he was out with me on either a hunting or fishing expedition. He was not a religious man in the normally accepted use of the term. Yet I have never met a man who was more conscious of God, or who lived by Christian principles like he did.

He was brilliant by many standards and there was no question about this. In the field of languages he was an accomplished linguist, speaking fluently in Norwegian, Swedish, German, English, Italian, and French and having a working knowledge of Arabic and the difficult language of Ethiopia—Amharic.

In addition to these qualifications, he was a mathematical wizard, a concert violinist, and a tenor of no mean accomplishment. As a boy of twelve, he had danced a command performance before the king of Norway.

During World War II, Bosse had been active in the Norwegian underground and he found a kindred spirit in me, with his undying hatred of anything that had to do with Communism.

Bosse's first job with the Ethiopian Government had taken him to a little city in southwestern Ethiopia near what is called the "Northwest Frontier." This place is well off the beaten path and can only be reached by plane. His home was a thatched roof house, built on stilts along the banks of a large river.

Many times, Aud told me about her trip to Ethiopia,

when she flew from her home in Oslo to marry this remarkable man. When she arrived in this jungle paradise, things were still pretty primitive. Shortly after her arrival, she went into the bedroom to freshen up. She stifled a scream, for there coiled up on the bed lay an eight-foot python. Bosse came at her call, to assure her the snake was harmless and was their official rat catcher. He pushed the coiled serpent off on the floor, where it slithered under the bed.

Shortly afterwards, sitting on the veranda sipping coffee, a half-grown black leopard stalked in. She said it deliberately looked her over with "hungry eyes," spit at her, and stalked out. The big cat followed Bosse around like a puppy. There were some new laws made in the Grythe family that day, one was that the menangerie would have to go, or Aud would be on the next plane bound for Oslo. Bosse wisely made the choice to keep her, although why he had any difficulty in making the choice, once you have seen Aud, was beyond me.

It was from this fascinating gal, that I received my first-hand information about Africa's "thick-hided" customers. During their two year stay in southern Ethiopia, one of Aud's favorite pastimes was to sit on the veranda and shoot the crocodiles which climbed up on the river banks to sun themselves.

"Ya," she said in her thick Norwegian accent, "I god so dot I could ged one wid every shod. You god to know where to poind de gun." She used a little 6.5 (25 caliber) Manlicher rifle.

The thick-skinned animals of Africa held a special fascination for me, as many of them were throwbacks to the dim ages when the mastodon and saber tooth tiger roamed the earth.

Crocodiles—those armored saurians with a generally ugly

disposition—predominated the thick-skinned animals of Africa as far as numbers were concerned. They are the greatest man killers in Africa and are a much greater menace than poison snakes. Almost all the streams and lakes in central Africa have crocodiles. Since people bathe in, or must cross these streams, the crocs are usually well fed.

I had a rather startling experience during my first trip to Sudan, which convinced me a person could not be too careful as far as crocodiles were concerned. We camped in a beautiful location on the banks of a small stream which normally emptied into the Blue Nile. It was the middle of the dry season and the little stream had dried up except for small pools which remained in sheltered places. Just below our camp was a pool which covered about five acres. It was kept fresh and cool by underground springs and was our water supply and bathing area. What wonderful relief it was to come in from a dusty day of hunting in the bush and be able to dip in the refreshing waters.

Before we went in for the first swim, we made a careful survey of the area, looking for signs of crocodile. As the stream bed itself was dry and we were some distance from the main river, the pond was pronounced safe. For ten days, this was our favorite spot. We supplemented our food supplies by catching delicious little catfish from our private lake. When we wanted to swim, we would strip on the edge of the pool, leaving our clothes and guns on the rocks which bordered the pool. One evening when most of us were merrily splashing in the cool water, Andy came down late. He stood on the north bank, which was almost twenty feet above the level of the pool and watched as we played in the water.

Suddenly we heard him shout. There was a note of real panic in his voice:

"Get the hell out of there, crocodile!" he yelled. For a moment I thought he was playing another of his practical jokes, but this idea was quickly dispelled when his rifle fired. Closely following his shot, there was a great deal of splashing, as something churned up the water near the edge of a huge boulder which bordered the pool. We headed for shore as fast as possible and I'm sure if there had been a timer there that day, some swimming records might have been set.

The camp boys waded into the bloody water and dragged a fourteen-foot crocodile ashore. How long that ugly reptile had lain in our pool was anyone's guess, but from then on we confined our bathing to the shallow water at the edge of the pool. Only the night before, I had swum alone in the pool and had dived off the same rock which had sheltered the croc.

One of the best places to see these reptiles is at Murchinson Falls, on the Nile River in upper Uganda. Thousands of crocodiles can be seen at one time. They are so thick in spots, as to be literally piled on top of each other. They make a curious sight, as they sleep with their gaping mouths wide open, while little birds walk around inside their mouths, cleaning food particles from their teeth. (A perfect answer to 34 per cent fewer cavities.)

When a crocodile is out of water, he is especially vulnerable and hunters can kill him easily. In the water it is a different matter, as he usually sinks to the bottom when he is fatally wounded.

Don't ever underestimate a croc out of the water though. He can move with amazing speed and a slap from his armored tail is almost as fatal as a bite from his big jaws. They are swift, silent killers in the water. They are found in unusual places. One day, I stopped at a little desert oasis which was at least fifty miles from any sizeable body of water. We found several eight-foot crocs in the little marsh which surrounded the oasis. How they had traveled over the fifty miles of hot sand I do not know.

In some places along the seacoast, huge salt-water crocs reaching a length of thirty feet are found. These are considered even more dangerous than the fresh water variety.

Crocodiles will eat anything. They will often creep up on native women doing their washing along the river banks. Children and dogs have often been knocked into the water by a blow from their tails. They will even attack hippos, and baby hippos are one of their favorite sources of food.

If the odds are right they will attack a rhino which is ten times their weight. They wait until the rhino enters the water to drink then seize him by a leg. Instead of trying to escape, which he could easily do by backing from the water, the stupid, stubborn beast tries to fight the croc. Every time he makes a pass at the croc, he is drawn farther into the water, until he is in over his head and drowned. The huge body is then dragged to the river bottom, where it is wedged under the limb of a tree and left to decompose. Crocodiles seldom eat fresh meat.

During the birthing season, hippos will systematically clear an area of the river to insure there are no crocs present to devour the "totos" (small ones). It is not unusual to see a baby hippo riding on his mother's back, as she swims slowly down the river. This is nothing more than a safety precaution which keeps the baby from becoming an item on the menu of some enterprising crocodile.

These reptiles lay up to sixty eggs in a nest which has been scooped out in the sand. The eggs which are not destroyed by birds, and by a little lizard which loves them, eventually hatch out in the heat of the sun. In spite of the natural odds against these reptiles and the fact they are hunted for their hides, they are one item in Africa which is not in danger of extinction.

The hippopotamus is another interesting water animal of Africa. He will provide hours of amusing and interesting observation. I have spent hours watching the antics of these "river horses" as they are called by the natives. The cows and calves love to play together and sometimes the the babies will climb on their mothers' backs and use them as a slide. Hippos are protected in most parts of Africa. One of the most interesting spots to see them is in the Kazinga channel, between Lake Edward and Lake George in Uganda. It is possible to get within feet of them, using a little care.

As you drift down the river in your boat, the hippos sunning themselves on the bank make a picturesque sight. When you get close to them, they will probably lumber down into the water with a big splash, until nothing remains of the herd but their knobby eyes and ears, which project above the water like periscopes.

Along with the hippos you will see hundreds of flame-colored flamingos, snowy egrets, long-legged storks, herons, and thousands upon thousands of ducks and Egyptian geese. Occasionally as you drift along, a hippo will bump against the bottom of your boat. There is little danger if your boat is sturdy. A bull hippo can easily overturn a native canoe and has even been known to bite them in two with a snap from his massive jaws. The big bulls are not to be fooled with. A big animal will weigh four tons, reach a length of fourteen feet, and stand five feet high at the shoulder. The tusks of his lower jaw may reach a length of twenty-seven inches and weigh almost nine pounds. The ivory in these tusks is softer than those of the elephant tusk and of less value.

The hippo is an accomplished swimmer. He can float

like a log and submerge at will. He can even run along the river bottom at eight miles per hour. It is not unusual for him to remain underwater for thirty minutes, but normally he only remains submerged for three or four minutes at a time. His valve-like nostrils close when he dives, and when he surfaces they open with a loud snort and blow a fine spray for a considerable distance.

Except for a few bristly hairs on the nose, head and tail, this animal is naked. He has a special skin mechanism which protects his skin when he comes out of the water into the sun. This mechanism secretes a thick, oily, pinkish sub-tance which keeps the hippo's hide from cracking. Some-times it appears as though the hippo is losing blood.

There are no hippos in the seasonal waters of Eritrea or Sudan, as they must have water the year around to re-main alive. If their hides dry out, they will die in a short period of time. There have been instances of hundreds of these animals dying during periods of drought in Uganda. The mud of the river becomes caked about their bodies until they are held in a cast the consistency of plaster of Paris. The hot sun cooks their flesh until it cracks open, or they are killed by predators who often eat them while they are still alive.

Most of the all-season streams of Central Africa have "river horses." They are particularly plentiful in the south, near the great lakes of Africa.

One of the most unusual thick-skinned animals in Africa is the rhinocerous. This three-toed throwback to prehistoric times is both bad tempered and dangerous. The rhino is one of the few animals in Africa which does not subscribe to the "you leave me alone, I'll leave you alone" theory. The thing which makes the rhino particularly dangerous is that he is so unpredictable. You never know for sure what he is going to do. An expert native guide can almost tell when a buffalo, lion, or hippo will charge. I have had them warn me: "That is far enough bwana, one step farther and he will surely charge." One time to test this, I took that extra step and had to run like the dickens to get to the Land Rover ahead of an irate buffalo.

When a rhino decides on action, it is amazing how fast he can move and how agile he really is. He will outrun a ten second halfback, or even a college sprinter. Usually, if a person keeps his wits about him, he can sidestep this headlong rush.

I talked with many experts, but never found one who could give me a satisfactory answer as to why the rhino is so belligerent. Some say it is because his eyesight is poor; others that he is lacking in brain power. The average rhino can't see too clearly beyond ten yards. If you approach from downwind, as any sensible hunter will do and he sees movement from the corner of his eyes, he will probably lower his head and come for you like a locomotive. He will even sound like a locomotive, huffing and chuffing in a realistic manner.

Rhinos are hated by all animals and most humans in the bush. They are the gangsters of the animal kingdom. They go to bed with a bad disposition and wake up on the wrong side of the bed every morning. When you meet a rhino, just depend on the fact he is going to have a bad disposition and you will be right more times than wrong. Even the elephants will avoid meeting them when possible. Many rhinos are killed each year on the Mombasa-Nairobi Railroad. If they happen to be on the track when a train comes along, they will lower their head and charge. There are things even a rhino can't defeat in combat and a railroad train is one of them. Sometimes, however, they will derail the train.

Unfortunately, this unique animal has been hunted almost

to extinction in spite of rigid game laws that are supposed to protect him. He is slowly being destroyed by poachers who kill the animal for its horns. For some reason, people of the Orient believe the horn of the rhino makes a wonderful aphrodisiac and pay fantastic prices for the ground horn. Just why people from this area need an aphrodisiac is beyond my comprehension, but the demand is cutting down on the supply.

The meat of the rhino is very tough, but the natives pound it between stones until it becomes palatable. At one time, the hide was in demand for the making of war shields. The hide, which will be between half and three-quarters of an inch thick, will make a shield when properly cured, which will turn a .30 caliber bullet fired from a hundred yards.

Occasionally a hunter will get a permit to kill one of these animals. Why a man would want to shoot one is beyond me, as they offer little real sport. I enjoyed seeing them blunder their way through the brush, though I can remember a few times when they scared the devil out of me. It was especially disconcerting to have one blunder into your camp area at night, for if they became frightened, they would run in a straight line, carrying tents and anything else along with them and trampling anything that got in their way. It was funny one night to see one of them running off with a tent draped over his horn. He was blinded and kept butting into trees. The man in the tent, although not hurt, thought differently and was scared half to death.

Rhinos usually feed in the late afternoon, breaking off small limbs from thorn bushes. They chew up the ends of the branches, spitting out the tough fibers. Even when the grass is tall and green, they prefer eating the tough branches of thorn trees.

An amusing incident took place on my first trip to Sudan

in 1960. The wife of one of our safari members had gone along with us. She was as fine a hunter as any man I ever met and had a lot of courage to go with it. She was also a whole lot more attractive than most of the male hunters. One day, she and her husband were out in their Land Rover, which was an older, cranky model, which gave them considerable trouble. They saw a rhino in the tall grass and decided to get some close-up pictures. Betty was driving and there was nothing she liked to do any more than drive right up under the nose of some wild animal.

When they were about thirty feet away, the big bull began to show signs of restlessness and Ray called for her to stop. The rhino was tossing its head from side to side, kicking up dust with its front feet and turning its big body around, with the horn stuck up like an antennae on a radar screen. Betty stopped the truck and turned off the engine so the vibrations would not disturb the picture taking. As the animal completed its turn, it suddenly saw the dim form of the truck ahead. Lowering its massive head, it came rumbling towards the truck, looking for all the world like some odd-shaped tank.

Thirty feet isn't very much space to cross and the cranky car didn't want to start. Ray was about to bail out, when the engine caught and Betty got underway. By this time, the big animal was so close that when he tossed his massive head, his horn caught under the rear frame of the Rover. With a mighty heave of his head, he lifted both rear wheels off the ground and dropped it with a resounding crash. The spinning wheels took hold with a sudden jerk and Ray went flying over the back of the seat, to land with a crash in the rear of the car, while the camera flew out of his hand. The impact caused the camera to open and the film was destroyed. They made an ignominious retreat with the rhino in hot pursuit. As usual their inconsiderate hunting companions though this was uproariously funny.

On this same trip, I came on a big rhino belly deep in the mud, surrounded by white tick birds. When the birds warned him, he headed for land, churning up the water and sounding like an overheated locomotive. A bushbuck, startled by the rhino, rushed away crying in alarm "Bau . . . bauuwh . . . bauuowwhhh!"

Of all the big animals, my favorite was the elephant. I never had any desire to shoot one of these wonderful beasts, although I had a lot of fun and some exciting moments taking pictures of them. The elephant can be a very worthy and dangerous adversary, but usually he is quite predictable and is a rather loveable fellow. The thing which fascinated me most about these animals was their trunk. It is their respiratory organ. When they hold it overhead, they can pick up the slightest odor and it is very difficult to get close to an old bull. The tip of the trunk is so sensitive it can pick up anything from a leaf to a large tree trunk. It is also used as a weapon and can deal smashing blows.

Elephants spend most of their time near water, like the hippo. They need this to keep their hides moist. The trunk is used as a hose to suck up water and it sprays its own hide and that of its fellows. It also uses the trunk as sort of a musical instrument, forcing air through this member in a loud trumpeting sound.

The tracks are easy to spot in soft ground, the feet of the female leaving an oval spoor, while those of the male are round.

My first experience with wild elephants came in 1959. When I speak of wild elephants, I refer to those which are found off the reservations. We were on safari, south of Barentu, near the Gash River in Ethiopia. I had seen and photographed elephants in British East Africa in 1958, both in Queen Elizabeth Park in Uganda and on the Amboseli Game Preserve at the foot of Mt. Kilimanjaro in Tanganyika. One can see hundreds of elephants in both these places. Still, elephants on the game reserve just don't seem the same as those seen in the wilds.

We had set up camp on the banks of the Gash River, which is one of the few all-season streams in northern Ethiopia. The first night in camp, a native runner from one of the villages came to tell us that a large herd of elephants had invaded a neighboring banana plantation. The head man of the village heard there was a party of white men close by and thought we might like to see the ceremony by which they got rid of the beasts. The opportunity to see this unusual ceremony, which I am sure has been seen by few white men, was too good to miss.

Andy was with me. We took one of the interpreters and with the native guide piled into my Land Rover for the trip to the village.

African hunting trails are nothing to brag about in daylight. At night, you literally take your life in your hands. This was especially true when anyone with the enthusiasm of Andy was behind the wheel. I always felt Andy was a frustrated racing driver for he had two speeds of travel, fast and faster. He would scoot over the veldt as if he was going to a fire and most of the time his passengers were on the floor instead of in the seats.

One of the hazards of driving on the veldt was the holes dug by such animals as wart hogs, aardvarks, and ant eaters. To hit one of these at forty miles an hour insured a good jolt, with the chance of overturning.

On this occasion, Andy beat me to the wheel and over my violent protests, which did not a bit of good, we took off in a cloud of dust. We bounced off down the narrow trail with the boys and I hanging on for dear life. As the headlights cut through the darkness, the track ahead looked like a tunnel in the night. Once, in a clearing, some large, tawny animal, probably a lion, leaped across the trail. Several times we saw the gleam of eyes in the headlights and once we passed close to a herd of gazelle who were grazing in a little meadow.

About an hour later, we began to hear the muted sounds of drums from ahead and knew we were reaching our destination. Everywhere you went in Africa you heard drums, even in the larger cities. I don't know if these were signal drums, but the natives seemed to know we were coming.

In a short time, we turned up a dirt road, which led between rows of tall palm trees. From ahead came the gleam of a great fire and soon we pulled into a clearing which was filled with hundreds of natives.

The village chief, a magnificent figure of a man came to greet us. He was over six feet four inches tall, a muscular man, naked to the waist. His only decorations were an amulet worn about his neck and a magnificent robe made from the skins of the colobus monkey, which was thrown over one shoulder. The villagers, both men and women, were gathered around the great fire, which shot flames thirty feet overhead. The people were naked except for tiny loin cloths of plaited banana leaves. It was evident they were about to dance.

The drums began again as we took our place before the fire, muted at first, and then with louder and more frenzied beats. The black skins of the drummers gleamed in the firelight. The dancers began to leap and cavort about the fire, the men waving spears with frightening abandon. On and on the dance went, hour after hour, while exhausted dancers fell to the ground; or men and women slipped away into the shadows which crowded close to the fire.

Suddenly, without warning the drums stopped. The quietness was almost unearthly. Then an old, old man, naked except for a moth-eaten colobus skin thrown about his shoulders, stalked into the circle of dancers. The little wizened old man reminded me of a wrinkled monkey. Still, there was an air of dignity and authority about him which was almost frightening. You could sense the fear in the natives and see the awe on their faces, as he stepped forward. He raised a withered hand and all sound ceased.

A small, naked boy, perhaps nine years old, was pushed forward into the circle. He did not appear reluctant or afraid, although something in the glaze of his eyes made me think he may have been drugged. The witch doctor threw some powder into the flames, which leaped up in momentary colored flames. The natives cowered back in obvious fear.

Taking a pot from the hands of his assistant, the old man began to smear some substance on the body of the boy, covering him from head to foot. Later I found this substance to be fresh elephant dung. I had heard of this being used by the pigmy elephant hunters of the Ituri Forest in Central Africa. These little men, covered with this disgusting mixture, were said to be able to stalk undetected under the bellies of the big beasts.

When the boy was thoroughly covered with the evil-smelling mixture, the witch doctor muttered some incantations and led him towards the banana fields. The villagers and their fascinated guests followed.

The moon was full, with only a few scudding clouds high overhead. The sight we saw was almost unbelievable. Moving among the banana plants was a herd of at least sixty elephants. Big bulls, heavy with ivory, were feeding on the tender plants, Cows, young bulls, and calves were scattered among the herd. There was no sound save the snuffling of the feeding animals and the occasional stomping of heavy feet.

The procession stopped about 300 yards downwind from the herd, while the witch doctor with the little boy walked slowly forward. When they were some fifty yards from the herd, the old man turned back and left the tiny figure of the boy standing alone, against the massiveness of the herd.

For a few seconds, the boy stood as though mesmerised, then he began to move slowly towards the herd. When he was about fifty feet from the herd, one of the big bulls noticed him for the first time. Slowly the huge cabbage ears spread out and the questing trunk came up until it was horizontal with the ground. You could almost read the thoughts going through the mind of the huge beast. We waited, holding our breaths, for it seemed certain the boy would be seized in a moment and battered to death.

"Maybe this is what we are to witness," I thought close to panic. "Maybe we are about to see a human sacrifice."

When the boy was within reach of the beast, he stopped. The huge beast began a systematic search of the tiny body, his trunk questing over the boy from head to foot. Then the huge ears went down and the bull turned back to his feeding.

We breathed a sigh of relief. Then an even more unbelievable thing happened. Walking up to the big bull, the boy took him by the trunk with both hands and lead him from the field. The rest of the herd followed behind, as docilely as a herd of tame cattle.

Africa never ceased to astonish me, for so many fantastic

things happened in everyday life, which somehow seemed to be commonplace. I knew my friends in the States would never believe many of the things I told them. Things happened which almost made one believe in the power of the witch doctors and their control over evil spirits.

It is common knowledge that elephants grow to an old age. Some possibly reach the age of a hundred years, although seventy seems to be a better average. There are many legends surrounding elephants, one of the more popular the one about "elephant graveyards." This is not true. The reason old elephants are seldom found is that they go off into almost impenetrable jungle to die. Sometimes they are escorted by two other big bulls, who stand on either side of the old bull and let him lean on them. They will even lift him to his feet with their tusks if he should fall. When they reach their destination, usually a place where food and water is close at hand, they leave the old fellow to die. He stays there until he becomes too feeble to feed and dies. Within a few days, the jungle scavengers will reduce his huge carcass to a pile of bones. Flood waters during the rainy season will deposit tons of silt over his skeleton and he will probably never be found.

Although elephants are seldom belligerent if left alone, they can be mighty destructive. The area where a large herd feeds will be pretty well devastated by the time they are through. They are vegetarians and need an enormous amount of feed to keep their huge bulks in operation. An expert told me they usually feed from sixteen to eighteen hours each day. Elephants in captivity will consume 150 pounds of dry feed and forty-five gallons of water at one meal. This will give you an idea of the immense amount of feed necessary to sustain a large herd. Wild elephants will eat as much as six hundred pounds of fodder in a twenty-four hour period. When they feed in the jungle, little damage is done, as the jungle grows quickly. When they come on cultivated land, the damage cannot be repaired so easily. Government hunters are often called into action to drive the animals from an area, or failing in this to kill them. Many elephants are killed every year in this manner.

In spite of this loss and of the loss from poachers who kill the animals for their ivory, the birth rate seems to keep up with the loss. This may seem surprising when you take into consideration the fact a female elephant will not begin to breed until she is from twelve to fifteen years old. The gestation period is about twenty-two months and the young are nursed for as long as two years. Because of their great life span, a normal female may give birth to five or six young during her life, even though she may only breed once every eight years.

The babies weigh about 75 pounds at birth and are pampered during their childhood.

There are few really large elephants left. A few years ago, a good pair of tusks might weigh 300 pounds or more. The record for a single tusk is 495 pounds, I believe. Today, the average is closer to a hundred pounds per pair. The high high cost of hunting these animals has kept down their destruction by sportsmen.

In spite of his bulk, and big bulls may weigh as much as six tons; an elephant can move through the thickest jungle like a gray ghost. He will travel through brush that seems impassable with scarcely the swish of a branch to mark his passing. His hide blends in perfectly with the background and sometimes a hunter can be within a few yards of an elephant and never detect him.

Elephants love water and you will often find them playing in it. They drink huge quantities, bathe in it, and love to squirt water over each other. In most areas where elephants bathe, the water becomes muddy. When this dries on their hide, it adds natural camouflage. The baby elephants love to play in the water and it is not unusual to see them using a muddy bank as a slide. One of the most amusing sights I ever saw was a huge bull, feeding deep in a swamp, covered with large blue and white water lilies which festooned his back and tusks.

In spite of his general good nature, this big fellow can be mighty tough when he becomes angry. His huge ears will stand out like cabbage leaves; his trunk will curl overhead and he will come for you like an express train. All the while he will be giving ear-splitting, trumpeting sounds. Unlike the rhino, he has excellent eyesight and a wonderful sense of smell. If he is wounded and allowed to get to his feet, he becomes exceedingly dangerous. In thick cover, he will often turn and stalk the hunter with great cunning.

Many people think the elephant's brain is large. It is really quite small in relationship to his size. As a result, many hunters using a head shot fire too high and hit the spongy bone above the brain. This causes little damage to the beast, but does a lot to increase his ire. Hunters caught by an elephant have been literally pounded into the ground. A white hunter in Uganda told me of seeing a native guide killed by a big bull. The animal caught the man in his trunk and slammed him against a tree. Then the broken body was hurled to the ground and the elephant kneeled on the body. Afterwards the bull methodically stamped the body into the ground. Then he dug a grave with his tusks and buried the body.

It is never advisable to underestimate a wild animal of any kind, for there will always be individuals who will not run true to form. Sometimes in the elephant family, you will run into a rogue, who because of his bad temper has been driven from the herd. This fellow, living by himself, hates everything that moves and will charge almost anything coming within his eyesight. Sometimes this bad temper is caused by an old wound, or an ulcerated tooth, or a tusk that gives him pain.

Many times elephants are most amusing. During my visit to Queen Elizabeth Preserve in Uganda, the natives were making a beer from maize called pombe. One native had made a barrel of beer and left the window of his hut open. There are many elephants on this preserve and it is not unusual to see them wandering among the native rondavels. There was an old, one-tusked elephant in this area, called affectionately, "Old George." George wandered into the native village and smelling the beer stuck his trunk through the window and consumed the entire barrel. If you have never seen a drunk elephant, you have missed something. "Temba" went on a drunken rampage. Reeling from side to side, he chased natives and tourists alike. He uprooted the garden around the lodge. He turned over the administrators' car. Finally when he began to tear down the native houses, they called in a conservation official, who shot the old boy.

Sometimes, if you are on the alert, you may see an old bull with heavy ivory resting his tusks in the crotch of a tree.

Another amusing sight is to see a big bull wrestling with a stubborn tree limb. He will grasp the pliant branch in his trunk, brace all four feet and pull with all his might. If the limb slips from his grasp, he will stamp the ground and trumpet in frustration.

The last of the thick-skinned African animals I want to mention here is the cape buffalo. "M'bogo," as he is called by the East African natives, is considered by many professional hunters to be the most dangerous animal in Africa. He is not only big and tough, he is also mean, and mighty hard to kill. He is nothing for an amateur to try and handle alone.

An aroused buffalo bull is as vindictive as a rhino, with a lot more brains behind his actions. The buffalo knows what he is doing at all times and it doesn't take the hunter long to find this out. He is one of the few animals who will track, ambush, and kill a hunter. Once he has been wounded and escapes into heavy brush, the hunter has a hard and dangerous assignment cut out for him.

At a distance, a herd of buffalo may look like domestic cattle, but this illusion rapidly disappears when you get closer. You can't help but admire this animal, for his very appearance is of tremendous vitality and strength. He is a huge creature, more than a ton of "angry pot roast" on the hoof and every pound of it seems to be made up of bone and muscle. His horns sweep out from the heavy, bony boss in the center of his head; which may be fourteen inches thick; and the tapered points, almost as sharp as a saber, may be over four feet apart. A really big bull will often travel with his head almost horizontal, so the massive horns rest on his withers.

Most natives are afraid of the buffalo. They make a great nuisance of themselves, eating and trampling down crops and killing the natives who are brave enough to try and stop them. There are few animals who will tangle with a big bull. White hunters told me that occasionally, a hungry, not very wise lion, will tackle one of these big bovines. Many times the battle royal ends in a tie with both opponents dead.

You hear all sorts of stories concerning this big fellow

from professional hunters. Most of them will agree, that a wounded buff is about the worst possible opponent to have when you are in heavy underbrush. He has a tremendous amount of vitality and if he regains his feet, after having been knocked down, there is trouble in store for the best hunter. Many times, he will backtrack, moving silently into ambush beside a game trail. When the hunter comes along looking for him, he will attack from ten feet or less. Like the elephant, he does a thorough job on any opponent he catches and there is little left when he is done.

A hunter in Dar Es Salaam told of an incident which took place near that city a number of years ago. A hunter had wounded a big bull, which chased him up a thorn tree. While climbing the tree, he dropped his rifle. The tree was small and the hunter could not get out of the buffalo's reach. Although the beast could not dislodge him, he reached up and with his file like tongue, began to lick the man's boots. After hours of licking, he had removed the boots and the man's flesh to the bone, up to his knees. The man's hunting companions found them both the next day. The hunter had tied himself to the tree with his belt, but had bled to death. The buffalo lay dead at the foot of the tree.

For all his bulk, he is fast and agile and can turn like a polo pony. You cannot dodge him as you would a domestic bull, for he charges with his head thrown back so he can watch your every move. Only at the last second will he lower his head for the toss. Coming head-on towards the hunter at thirty miles an hour, he offers a poor target. A high-powered bullet fired between his horns will usually bounce off the horny structure. The only shot available is at the point of the nose. If this is delivered accurately, it will break his spine and end the contest right there. The best shot, if available, is at the point of the shoulder. A large caliber bullet should be used and it should have a solid point, as it may have to travel through eighteen inches of tough muscle. A softnosed bullet will flatten out before it reaches bone. I would advise using a rifle of at least .375 caliber, although I did quite well with a .338 magnum, which delivers almost exactly the same muzzle velocity with a 250-grain bullet. I'm convinced the best weapon to use against this tough animal is the Winchester African, a .458 caliber magnum which fires a 500-grain bullet at tremendous speed. It is also within the price range of most hunters, as you can buy one for less than $500. The beautiful English double rifles, which are without doubt the best big game weapons available, may cost as much as $2,000.

I had several interesting experiences with buffalo. The first was in Kenya in 1958. We were on the Amboseli Preserve and had stopped to take pictures of some animals who were grazing. Strict regulations forbid visitors from dismounting from their vehicles in the presence of dangerous animals, so I was doing my shooting from the back of a Land Rover. We drove up to within fifty yards of the herd. As we got close, I noticed the bulls turned to face us, while the cows and calves went into the protection of the semicircle formed. One big bull in the center of the line began to toss his head and kick dust over his shoulders. I had lived on a ranch long enough to know what this means and recognize it as a danger signal.

About this time, a little Morris Minor drove up with two elderly English ladies aboard. They seemed anxious to get pictures, for one of them, ignoring the frantic signals of my guide, hopped blithely from the car and began to grind away. Just as she got going good, the big bull gave a snort, pawed up some more turf, and headed for the old ladies.

Seeing she was the target, the woman ran screaming for her car. Luckily her friend had the engine running and they got underway just in time, departing in a cloud of dust, with the bull in mad pursuit. Every time he jumped after the fleeing car, he let go with a blood-chilling bellow and hooked viciously at the rear of the car. Fortunately he never made it, or there is no doubt he would have demolished the car and the two little old ladies.

The buffalo was one animal I enjoyed hunting, for he was a worthy opponent who gave as much as he got. I can't remember a single time I went into tall grass or heavy brush after one of these animals that my heart didn't beat faster and my mind stir with a breath of fear. It was the most exciting sport I had ever taken part in.

On our second Sudan trip, we got two fine bulls and I was in on the kill of both of them. The first, I got early one morning, when I went out with my guide and found three of them near a water hole. The wind was just right and we were able to get within thirty-five yards or so. From there I busted the largest with a 250-grain solid point, which broke his front shoulder. He dropped as though he had been poleaxed, while the other two took off into the brush. I busted him again to be safe. He was a magnificent specimen, with huge black horns which measured forty-seven and a half inches. The only trouble is to find a wall big enough to hang him on.

Two days later, I helped stop another big bull. This time is was a different story. Maybe because I had dropped the first one with so little trouble, I was a bit over confident. I lost this confidence in a hurry. Joe, Willy, Andy, and myself went out early that day. Jim and Willy were carrying .375 magnums. They went around one side of a thicket where we saw signs of the beasts. Andy armed with a .300

Weatherby and I with my .338 magnum took the other side. We had scarcely lost sight of our companions when two shots rang out. We turned just in time to see an amazing sight. At any other time, it would have been highly amusing. Now it wasn't a bit funny. Coming toward us at a dead run were our two doughty hunters. About thirty yards behind came one of the biggest, blackest, maddest bull buffaloes I had ever seen. With every leap, he cut down the distance between him and his fleeing targets. With every jump he gave out a blood-chilling bellow.

I guess Andy and I gaped for a second before swinging into action. We fired almost together. At the sound of the shots, followed instantly by the meaty smack of the big bullets striking heavy flesh, the buff staggered and went to his knees. We frantically jacked shells into the chambers of our guns, for he was up instantly. Blowing bloody froth from both nostrils he came for his new target, us. Again the two rifles fired as one and again he went down, to bounce up like a rubber ball. For the third time we fired, our rifles joined this time by Willy's .375. The big bull went down to stay. He was so close, I could take a long step forward and touch him with the barrel of my gun. Too darned close by any standard.

When we checked the carcass, we found seven bullet holes in his front shoulders, any one of which could have killed him. There were two indentations in his boss where heavy bullets had struck and bounced. Looking at that huge massive machine of destruction, I suddenly found my legs too weak to carry my weight and I had to sit down.

From that time on, I never underestimated any animal I hunted.

9 Forest Primeval

For bird lovers, Africa is a paradise of color and excitement. Days can be spent doing nothing but viewing and photographing some of the most beautiful and unusual birds to be found anywhere in the world.

By the same token, a "shotgun man" can have a field day, spending as many hours as he desires, shooting birds for use as food in the hunting camp. There is no more appreciated menu than one which contains guinea fowl or francolina. I never went on a field trip without taking my smooth bore with me. Many times when I became bored with the regular day's schedule, I'd slip off with my shotgun to get some meat for camp. Often I'd end up by sitting beside some waterhole to watch the birds which came in what seemed to be never-ending numbers. Bird hunting has a special thrill all its own; the excitement which comes with a pair of whirring, fast-beating wings overhead.

Birds are found in great abundance in all parts of Central and East Africa, with the exception of the desert areas. Noisy guinea fowl, delicious francolina, sand grouse, and the fast-moving mourning dove can be seen by the tens of thousands every day in the field. It would hardly seem right to wake on a frosty morning in a hunting camp, without the plaintive cry of the mourning dove ringing in your ears, as it flies back and forth between the palm trees. The water holes would not be the same if it were not for processions of guinea fowl, as they march with almost military precision to the water.

Many of Africa's birds are exotically beautiful in their brilliant plumage. These are in direct contrast to others which are hideous to the extreme. The Great Hornbill is a good example of this. He wins human approval, not for his beauty, but because he is an energetic snake killer.

This ugly, ungainly bird, is big by any fowl standards, standing four feet tall and with a wingspread of seven feet. He can still be seen in some remote areas of Ethiopia, although his numbers have steadily diminished over the years. His plumage is the black of an understaker's suit, brightened by the snowy white of his breast, which looks something like a formal vest. He has a huge, scissor-shaped bill, which may be three feet long and five inches wide, with serrated edges which look like the teeth of a saw. The beak is set above a huge goiter which is brilliant red on the male and bright blue on the female. The black feathers are long and coarse. His legs are large scaly sticks, ending in strong claws. Above the beak, and attached to it, is a bony, prominent protuberance which sticks out like the air scoop on an airplane. When you see one of these monstrosities in flight you might think for a moment you were seeing some miniature prehistoric flying monster.

These birds mate for life and if either of them dies, the other will not remate. Because of their scarcity, they are rigidly protected by the game laws. On rare occasions, you may be lucky enough to see one in flight, holding a writhing snake in its beak. They will tackle any of the poisonous serpents, shuffling before the angry reptile in a sort of grotesque dance. They carry their wings spread across their breast as a shield against the snake's desperate lunges.

Another snake killer found in this same area is the secretary bird. This fellow has long plumes which project from the back of his head, like the quills from behind the ears of an old-time secretary; hence the name. He is slate gray and black in color.

His long scaly legs and loose plumage afford good protection against the poisonous snakes it preys on. In some places, the bird is tamed and kept as an aid in controlling snakes and rodents around the garden areas of a home.

Most of the brilliantly colored birds are found in the warm equatorial regions of southern Ethiopia, Sudan, and East Africa. One of the most prolific areas, insofar as numbers are concerned, is the great lakes area of Africa and along the southern portions of the Nile River. Here the brilliant, flame-colored flamingos can be seen in huge flocks, along with the lovely snowy egret, herons of all types, parrots of all sizes and colors, and vast flocks of Egyptian geese and ducks.

Probably the most interesting bird of Africa is the ostrich which is the largest of existing birds. A mature bird will reach a height of seven feet and weigh up to three hundred pounds. He can run faster than a horse. I have cruised beside them at sixty miles per hour without seeming to disturb them a great deal. Their three-toed feet can deliver a kick like that of a mule and along with their big beak are used quite effectively in defense and offense. The story about ostriches burying their heads in the sand on seeing danger approach is another of those fables which has developed down through the centuries.

When the birds are nesting, the eggs will be guarded

alternately by the male and female. If you happen to come close to the nest, the nesting bird will try and decoy you away by limping off with a wing and leg dragging, as though it were crippled.

Single ostrich eggs may weigh three and a half pounds and will make a delicious omelet which compares to one made with two dozen hen eggs.

One day, I sat spellbound as I watched a young chick trying to break his way through the tough shell of an egg. First I heard the "tick, tick, tick" of the chick's beak. Finally a crack appeared and the chick began to enlarge this with its beak until finally its head was outside. Then the struggle became almost violent, as the young bird attempted to escape the confines of the shell. It worked until exhausted; rested for a few minutes and then continued the struggle. Within an hour after I heard the first tick, the chick was walking, wet and weak, but triumphant, outside its prison. An hour later, it could walk without a wobble and when I came back the next day, it could run faster than I.

Ostriches are getting quite rare now and are closely protected. In Ethiopia, the fine is $1,000 ($250 U.S.) for killing one of the birds. When ostrich feathers were the vogue during the gay nineties, the birds were pursued by hunters mounted on horse back, who, riding in relays, would pursue the birds until they fell exhausted. The males were clubbed to death so the feathers would not be splattered with blood. As it takes the male several years to achieve the full spendor of its plumage, if the finest males are slaughtered, it becomes a deadly blow to the survival of the species.

During this same period, flocks of egrets, which bear the lovely osprey feathers during the mating season, were killed until they dwindled almost to the point of extinction. As the birds were killed in the breeding areas, their young were left to starve to death and it became the old story of "killing the goose that laid the golden egg."

One of the most unique experiences a man can have in Africa is a journey into one of the great rain forests of Central Africa. It is not the most pleasant jouney one can take, but it is different from anything you will find anywhere else on the continent. These forests are usually found on the lower slopes of rugged mountain ranges, such as the Ruwenzori's which stand guard between Uganda and the Congo.

After the rains have ceased, the approaches to these mountains are covered with lush green grass as tall as a man's head. There will be little game about now, for the antelope and gazelle move to higher ground to escape from the predators who roam in the tall grass. Crossing the vast plains towards the forests is a thing to delight the soul of man at this time of the year. You will find huge areas, covering thousands of acres, which will be ablaze with the brilliant orange of tiger lilies in full bloom. Close by there may be an equally large area covered with the gorgeous color and fragrance of Easter lilies, while another area adjoining these two may be covered with white morning glories which are highlighted by brilliant purple centers.

Once you have entered the forest, everything changes rapidly and the thick foliage seems to literally swallow you up. Your pace slows to a crawl. You must climb over the trunks of fallen forest giants which may be twenty feet or more in diameter. In other places you must crawl under the trunks or projecting limbs. Along the narrow trail, thorns of all types reach out to grasp you by the clothing. Some like the "wait-a-bit" thorn are so tenacious they must be cut from your clothing with a sharp knife. Nettles, which tower over your head, will sting your hands and face and giant ferns will slap against your body. The clinging loops of lianaa, hanging from the trees overhead, will wrap around your body like tenacious serpents, and will have to be cut loose.

No matter where you look, there will be nothing to be seen but rich, verdant green. The roof overhead will be green, the walls of the forest are green, the carpeting of the jungle is green, and even the sickly light which filters down through the thick foliage will be a thick, greenish hue.

Underfoot will be the eternal ooze and slime of primordial days; the odor of rotting vegetation which will be repugnant to your nostrils. Mixed with this stench will be the cloyingly sweet odor of the multitude of tropical flowers which grow overhead and which will somehow remind you of a funeral parlor.

There are insects to consider too. Insects which sting through the thickest khaki clothing and which cling to every exposed particle of skin, greedily sucking away at your blood supply. Our guide told us:

"One of those bloody bugs sucked so much of my blood last year, he sent me a card on Father's Day."

If when you stop to rest you make the mistake of sitting down on a rotting log, you will probably find yourself covered with safari ants whose bites are red hot. The effects of these bites will remain with you for twenty-four hours.

Maybe you will find that ticks have gotten past the barrier you thought you had erected with insect repellant, when you followed directions and applied it to your belt line and the top of your socks. Every chance possible, you will check your body for these troublesome little pests. They like to get between the toes, where they burrow in and must be dug out with the point of a sharp knife, taking care that the heads are removed or there is danger in infection. Sometimes, they can be persuaded to let go and back out, if you will hold a lighted cigarette to their rear ends.

At other times, while crossing a particularly muddy spot,

you may sink to your waist in the stinking ooze. When you reach higher ground, you will probably find your legs covered with dozens of slimy leeches. These must be pried off and their circular bites treated with iodine.

As we get deeper and deeper into the forest, we begin to see signs of wild life. The noise overhead will become incessant as parrots try and outdo the monkeys in their clamor. Up ahead, a long, slim, black snake slithers across the path, probably a deadly mamba.

Slipping and slithering across the rotting logs, sometimes gagging at the fetid odors which came up from swamp gasses underfoot, a parrot screeched close overhead and others took up the cry. They seemed to be mocking my awkwardness.

Finally after struggling for several hours, we came to a clearing where some forest giant had succumbed to the elements or the ever-present termites and had crashed to the ground. Two hundred feet overhead, we could see a small patch of blue sky. I stopped to examine some lovely orchids which hung from a vine and was surrounded by a cloud of huge, brilliantly colored butterflies which fluttered among the vines in a macabre dance.

At times, one can walk though the forest, with the only sound, that made by your footsteps. Then as though at a signal, the whole forest erupts into a cacophony of sound and turmoil. Birds screech and scold in the green depths overhead and hordes of black and white colobus monkeys in their bishop's mantles join in the bedlam as they swing from limb to limb far above.

Off the trail, you may hear the crashing sounds made by some large beast and your heart seems to come into your throat, while you wonder if it might be caused by an irate rhino or a rogue elephant. If one should appear, there is no place for you to go. In some places the vegetation becomes so thick, the only way you know if you are going up or down hill is by the tilt of your body.

Along the trail you may see footprints the size of a wash tub, with huge piles of still-smoking droppings nearby. The guide motions excitedly into the forest and you hear the word "tembu" repeated over and over again and know an elephant is nearby.

Far ahead, you hear the rumbling of sound which may be like that of an approaching freight train. It grows nearer and soon the tree tops far overhead begin to whip in the grip of a fierce wind. Lightning flares and thunder rolls in deafening explosions. Somewhere close by, a forest giant crashes. Then the rain comes down in torrents which threatens to drown you. You can't even see the guide who is only a few yards up the trail. You stop and try to get some shelter beside a huge tree. Then as suddenly as it began, the rain stops and you hear the thunder as it goes rolling away from you. In a few more minutes the forest is awake with sound again.

The jungle people have ideas of taste and smell which are much different from those of the white men. They will follow the odor of decaying meat for hours, until they find the carcass of a dead elephant. Then they will gorge on the putrid meat until they can scarcely walk. They eat grubs, snakes, bats, and most types of insects. As long as it is edible, the native will eat anything. They seem to have a digestive system which will rival that of a crocodile. On many occasions, I have seen native guides cut a piece of bleeding meat from the freshly killed carcass of an animal just shot and eat it raw with evident relish. They eat the livers and intestines of an animal while they are still warm from body heat.

One of their favorite foods is wild honey. When they find

a bee tree, they use vines, much as a telephone repair man uses his safety belt, and scurry up the tree for a hundred feet. Reaching the honey comb, they cram handfuls of honey and comb into their mouths, while the bees swarm about them. They never seem to be stung.

Most of the jungle people seem to be shy and gentle, although in the old days, I was told, the pigmy people of Central Africa were fierce cannibals.

I was only in the deep forest for two days, but that was quite enough for me. When we reached the edge of the jungle and saw the sunlight, it was one of the most welcome sights I can recall.

As we came from the edge of the forest, we were met by a local game commissioner. He had arrived at a nearby village the day before to shoot a rogue elephant which had been giving the villagers trouble. The meat from the beast had been distributed to the villagers.

"We had a slight accident yesterday," he said, "one of of the natives who were cutting up the animal was inside the carcass. A rather energetic chap on the outside stabbed him as he worked. A bloody shame."

The workers were laying around in the shade, blood spattered and in a state of stupor.

"Beer?" I asked.

"No, those chaps must have eaten seven or eight pounds of raw elephant meat," he continued. "Sometimes the manoumi (men) will gorge themselves and then go out and force themselves to regurgitate so they can eat more. Bloody peculiar, eh what?"

I had been fortunate to never encounter safari ants in any of my travels. The commissioner told me they had become somewhat of a problem in his area.

"Everyone is afraid of the bloody bugs," he said. "When

they pass through the country, they travel in a path eight to ten inches wide and devour any bloody thing which is alive in their path. I saw a crippled cow which had been stripped clean. The blasted bugs will do it in seconds too. When they come into a village the WOGS usually clear out."

Now that we were out of the forest, we began to see many more game birds. Guinea fowl were as thick as fleas on an old hound dog. One evening, I stood on the hood of the Land Rover and counted eleven flocks nearby. Each flock must have numbered over a thousand birds. In some areas they scratch up a hundred acres of land, until it appears as though some farmer has worked it over with a hoe.

The African guinea fowl is an exact replica of his American cousin. In fact this bird was introduced to the New World from East Africa. His breast meat is delicious. Although we never served it under glass, guinea breasts marinated overnight in a sauce made from sour cream was a gourmet's delight.

Another interesting game bird is the francolina. This bird, which resembles our grouse, is cursed by the fact that he is all white meat, which will rival that of pheasant as far as taste is concerned. The African bustard is also found in large numbers. This large bird, which resembles a crane, tastes like our American wild turkey. It sports a full feathered crest, a pompom on its throat, and polka dot wings with a long tail. The sand grouse which can be found by the tens of thousands is small but bullet fast and is a real challenge to the smooth bore gunner, along with the mourning dove.

Several times Andy and I shot guinea exclusively for food, to feed large numbers of people. Preparing for a rather unusual banquet at the NCO Club, we shot 187 birds in one day. It was not unusual to kill five birds with one shot and Andy held the record by dumping seventeen.

One day, when we were hunting guinea for camp food, we were driving a rather old jeep which was not in the best of mechanical condition. We usually hunted guinea with a vehicle, as they were worse than pheasant when it came to running on the ground and it was difficult to get close enough to them on foot. We would drive among the thorn bushes until we sighted a flock, then try and drive as close as possible before firing. With a little practice, we could tell when they were about to take off; then we would stop the jeep, dismount, and fire away.

We were in fast pursuit of a large flock which was heading for the shelter of some thorn bushes nearby. When we were about ten feet from the thicket Andy applied the brakes with no result and we crashed head on into the thick brush. I was wearing shorts that day and the windshield was down. Seeing a large limb, armed with three-inch spikes slashing at my face, I put up my foot to try and deflect it. I succeeded in forcing it away from my face, but it slipped off my boot, raking the full length of my leg. The thorns bit deep into flesh and muscle and I was lifted bodily from the front seat to land with a crash in the rear of the vehicle. When we were finally able to extricate ourselves, we were a mess, scratched and bloody from head to foot. I got the worst of it by far, as my bare legs and back were a bloody mess, cut to ribbons. Some of the thorns had become imbedded as deep as two inches and it took us a full two hours to dig out the broken points. These thorns were dangerous, as the green thorns would fester and start an infection within hours if they were not removed.

As in most circumstances, Andy saw some humor in this situation. It gave his fertile mind the idea for a wonderful hunting story. When we got back to camp, he told this story:

"Jack was sitting by a water hole up in that country north of Hadundami, you know the place," he said with a perfectly straight face, "when a big leopard crept up on him and jumped him. The old man fought that damn cat off with a knife." To prove his story, he would show them the deep scratches on my body, which certainly looked convincing. Do you know, there were a surprising number of people who believed that story and it became another of those stories which is told over and over again in hunting camps and which becomes better with each retelling. This is the first time I've ever confessed it was a "put-up job."

10 Record Book Trophy

Not every man is lucky enough to realize some of his life-long ambitions. I was about to realize one of mine, as I lay on a sun-baked ridge of mountains in northern Eritrea.

Lying in the scant shade from the acacia tree, I had been scanning the opposite side of the valley for some time with by binoculars. Off to the right, my hunting companion, Andy Ford, was doing the same thing. We were looking for that most majestic of all the big antelopes, the fabulous spiral-horned antelope called the greater or major kudu. This antelope is one of the largest and surely the most stately of this family which numbers many species. The kudu has sometimes been called the "antelope king." In their dance of triumph when they have killed a lion, certain tribes of East Africa use the spiral horn of a kudu as a sort of trumpet.

This beautiful animal stands close to six feet at the front shoulder and a big bull will weigh seven hundred pounds. Their imposing horns which rise in corkscrew swirls from the animal's head will sometimes reach a length of five feet or more. This animal is found only in the highlands of East Africa. The closest most people get to a kudu, including a lot of kudu hunters, will be in some game preserve, for this animal is extremely timid and elusive. To see the animal in its wild state, it is necessary to head for the scrub-covered rocky hills, where the big antelope can climb like a mountain goat. He is blessed with wonderful eyesight and an extremely sensitive sense of hearing. This plus the camouflage of his striped gray coat makes him difficult to spot. The hunter is lucky indeed who looks at a trophy bull through the sights of his rifle.

The kudu has long been high on the list of big game trophies and for a time, a few years ago, headed the list. His mounted head makes a lovely trophy. The horns are fashioned in the form of wide open spirals of up to four turns. The cows have no horns. The body of the animal is grayish brown, with vertical white stripes along the sides. The face has white markings on the nose and cheeks and around the eyes. The ears are large, the tail long and tufted, and they sport a fringe of hair around their throats.

I had been in Eritrea for almost two years by now, and for most of this time, I had been trying vainly to get a hunting permit for kudu. A special permit was necessary, which bore the signature of the chief executive. This was like having to obtain a written permit from the President of the United States. Fortunately, through my duties as Game Warden, I had met a number of officials in the Agriculture Department. These were the men who had the responsibility to see that Eritrean game laws were enforced. One of these officials was a good friend of mine. He in turn had a friend, whose cousin worked in the office of the chief executive. Through the good offices of this man, plus a little help from a few Ethiopian dollars which were wisely spent, I got these important papers. Standing with the permit in my hands, I felt like a little boy who has just got his first rifle.

One of the best kudu areas in Eritrea was relatively close

to Asmara, so the cost of a hunting trip was low. There was no expensive safari necessary, no air travel to Ethiopia from the States, very little red tape for which Ethiopia is famous.

I had been on several hunting trips by this time, so I asked Andy Ford to go along with me. Not only was he my favorite hunting companion, he was also a first-class mechanic and this of itself was important when going into the back country. In addition, he had hunted this area before and had shot a fine kudu there a few years before. I could handle a hunting car with the best of drivers and chase gazelle across the plain at near top speed, thanks to some experience I had in auto racing, but the innards of the mechanical animals baffled me. Andy could coax the most cranky vehicle into doing anything he wanted and all he needed was a screw driver, a pair of pliers, and some wire.

Because the hunting area was so close, we decided to keep our equipment to a minimum and travel in one vehicle. A friend of ours had a Dodge power wagon which he was willing to lend us at no cost, if we would replace the engine for him. He had the new engine, but needed the mechanical help. We agreed to do the job and every night for a week, Andy and I worked long after midnight getting the truck in working order. Finally on Friday morning, we finished the work and went out for a test run.

We were just in time, for we had planned our trip for that weekend. When Andy suggested we try out luck over a weekend, I was surprised. I had read stories of men who had hunted on safari for several weeks, looking for a trophy kudu.

"If those men with professional guides needed weeks to produce a trophy, how in the world will we get one in three days?" I thought. I had enough faith in Andy, though that I was willing to take the chance.

Our camp crew was made up of Fadul Gasim, the Moslem cook who wasn't sidetracked by his religious beliefs to the extent where he would spoil a wild pig roast; Cookie, who went along as a skinner; and Mohammed, a local boy from the Cheren area, who had been out with Andy many times and who could speak the local language.

Early Friday afternoon, we managed to slip away from work a bit early. The truck was packed and ready and all we needed to do was sign out at the Guard House. We planned on staying at the Rest Hotel in Cheren over night and leaving early for the hunting area which was about fifty miles north of Cheren.

Evening travel in Eritrea is interesting. The heat of the day is beginning to dissipate; the shadows thrown by the rocks make fantastic shapes on the road; and a cool breeze begins to blow in from the mountains.

As we topped the first ridge on the plateau, we saw stretched far to the west of us, the fantastic peaks of the mountains which ring in Mansura Valley and which range west and north toward Agordat and the Sudan border. The sun, sinking in the west, painted the mountains with gorgeous colors of red, rose, and orange, which were reflected in the fleecy clouds that sailed serenely overhead in a sky of azure blue.

Along the road, natives were hurrying towards their homes. This is the only time of the day when you see the natives hurry. I don't know whether they are in a hurry for their evening meal, or whether they are afraid of the dark. I rather suspect the latter, for this is when the evil spirits roam in the form of hyenas and even savager shiftas.

Everywhere you see the white-robed figures hurrying to their houses, while from the villages comes the aromatic smell of cooking fires being fed with eucalyptus wood.

This is one time of the day when Eritrea is silent. The

only sound which will be heard is the occasional broken-hearted bray of some donkey, or the lowing of some cow waiting to be milked. In a little while, the crickets and frogs will take up their evening melody, to be joined, as darkness falls, by the sharp barking of the jackal and the hideous laughing cry of the hyena.

The road drops over the escarpment and falls rapidly away in one breathtaking, hairpin turn after another. The breeze becomes warmer and softer. We pick up our shotguns and check their loads. Our conversation becomes desultory, for we are on the lookout for white-robed figures which may materialize at any time from the rocks, like bandits descending on a stagecoach in the Old West.

In a little while, the lights of Cheren are seen in the distance and we breathe a sigh of relief and relax a little. In a few more moments, we drive through the crowded streets of the little city and turn off into a side road which takes us through the gates into the hotel compound. The native boys are sent downtown for their suppers, while we relax in the warmth and hospitality of the hotel.

The Rest Hotel in Cheren is a lovely spot. The building is built on classic Italian lines and looks much like a villa. The stucco building has a screened-in veranda on three sides and you can sit outside in the mellow air, enjoying the fragrance from a multitude of tropical flowers that cover the walls and roof of the building. Here bougainvillaea, frangpani, and honeysuckle vie in perfuming the evening air. To the rear of the little dining room is a patio with a small pool and behind this are clay tennis courts. Farther to the rear is a tropical fruit garden with orange, lemon, and papaya trees. The food is good.

After a hearty meal and a short visit with the genial manager while we smoke our after dinner cigars, we are ready for bed. We will be up before daylight tomorrow and one of the cooks will prepare a delicious breakfast to hasten us on our way. We hit the soft beds and go to sleep with visions of enormous kudus chasing us in our sleep.

Early morning in Cheren always fascinated me. Not only was the air clean and soft, but special aromas seem to be present which you do not notice later in the day. The fragrance of the flowers mixed with the spicy odor of the citrus trees, blending into something wonderful and out of this world. You do not need an alarm clock to wake you here, as the call to the faithful comes ringing out from the minaret of the local mosque, which towers over the market place, calling the faithful to worship. The Moslems flock from their homes to place their prayer rugs and bow down towards Mecca in worship. The shrill cry of the muzzeim rings out over the city: "Allahuk bar!-A'shadadu la ilah-il allah! wa Mohammed er-rasool allah!" God is great! I testify there is no God but God and Mohammed is His Prophet!" In the distance you hear the sounds of crowing cocks and the braying of donkeys who complain because they face another day of work.

In a little while, everything is in readiness. Canteens have been filled with fresh, cold water. Breakfast has been finished and the cook appears with your lunch which is made up of sandwiches and fruit. Not the delicate little sandwiches you get in restaurants, but hearty, man-sized ones, where the ham is sliced thick, with even thicker slices of cheese. In a few minutes the engine of the power wagon fires up and we are on our way north out of the city.

This is my first trip into this area and already I am seeing new sights. We are in the heart of the citrus growing area of Eritrea. Row on row of these trees stand brilliant in their glossy greenery, filling the air with their delicious, spicy aroma.

For the first hour we pass through these groves, then the

dirt road begins to wind up and up to the 11,000-foot pass over the mountains. On the lower reaches of the mountain, we pass huge olive trees, with trunks thirty feet in diameter, which must have been here when Christ was born.

At the foot of the pass, we come to a causeway across a little river. Now the stream is only a trickle but at one end is a pond which covers possibly an acre of land.

"Let's stop and fish here a bit," Andy said.

I was a bit unhappy with this suggestion, as I was anxious to get to the hunting area and our time was so short.

Andy stopped to explain to me, a bit sarcastically.

"I want to reach a certain spot at eleven o'clock," he said. "I thought I'd show you something unusual while we were here."

He had insisted we bring along our casting rods, which seemed stupid to me. How in the world would we go fishing in the middle of an arid place? I was about to find out.

We baited up the hooks with liver and soon were pulling in fighting catfish up to twenty-four inches in length. They looked a bit different than our Stateside catfish, as their bodies were sort of like eels. Andy explained how these fish lived in the mud at the bottom of the rivers. When the water dried up during the dry season, they would burrow in the wet sand, until the rains came again and they could come up to spawn. In Kenya these fish are called "gumboi." I have seen natives dig them out of the wet sand, when the riverbed appeared to be completely dry.

After getting a mess of fish for dinner and placing them on ice, we headed northwards once more.

We were headed for an area known as Cub Cub, located near the village of Nagcfa and close to the Sudan border. We were in a little valley now, still at high altitude. The scenery had changed little—the same type of cactus was present and the same acacia trees. As we approached a little knoll that projected into the valley, Andy stopped the truck.

"Let's go up there and look around," he said, pointing to a rocky ledge above the road, "I've got a hunch we may see something of interest up there."

I knew we were wasting our time.

Leaving the truck in the shade of a big tree, we moved out, carrying our rifles and binoculars. After a thirty-minute climb which seemed to be straight up, we arrived breathless and wet with sweat. We threw ourselves down in the shade of an acacia tree. About six hundred yards away, across a little valley, another slope climbed up to be lost in the fleecy clouds which hovered overhead.

Focusing my glasses on the opposite side of the valley, I saw the first of them: dark, grayish-brown animals, larger than our American elk, they stood out in sharp relief.

"Relax," said Andy, "they are only cows and calves."

There were eight cows and calves in the little clearing across the valley. The cows were hornless, but two of the calves had begun to grow horns which might someday grace the wall of some lucky hunter's den.

"Watch close now," Andy said, "there may be some big bulls close about."

We lay there for close to thirty minutes, scanning every inch of the opposite slope. Then I heard him curse under his breath. Andy was not a man given to profanity and I knew he must have seen something of interest.

"Jack," he said in a whisper, as though afraid his voice might carry across the valley, "look at that big bastard over there."

I followed his pointing finger, until I could pick up the form of an enormous kudu which had just grazed around a bend in the mountain trail some 800 yards away. His horns curved up and back for a good three and a half turns. In the glasses he looked gigantic. My first impression was that he appeared to be in flight, even though he was standing still. Every few seconds, he would raise his head and scan the hillside alertly looking for anything that might represent danger, listening to catch the slightest foreign sound.

It came to me that we were very fortunate to find such a wonderful trophy so soon. I also realized our work had not even commenced.

We began a painstaking stalk to get within range of this great beast. Crawling over rocks which were almost too hot to touch, the sharp edges of the lava rocks cut into our knees and hands. Hordes of sticky, bloodthirsty camel flies settled on our hands and faces and sweat ran into our eyes. It was a course in torture. Cactus spines clutched at our clothes and we had to move with extreme caution, not only because we didn't want to alert the animal, but because we were in the natural habitat of poisonous snakes.

Time and again, it seemed as though we would get into range of the big bull, only to have him drift off ahead of us.

Crossing a little rise, we finally got within five hundred yards of him. It was getting on into the day, so Andy decided to take a shot at him with his .300 H&H magnum. The big gun had the range and power to make a killing shot at this distance. Distances, however, are deceptive in the clear mountain air, especially when shooting down hill, even when using a telescopic sight. I watched through my binoculars, while Andy squeezed off a careful shot. A split second later, the big bull appeared to stumble, then recovered and with his horns laid back along his withers, he disappeared under a full head of steam.

"That's the last we'll ever see of that baby," was Andy's gloomy prophecy.

When we reached the spot where he stood, we found blood splashes on the rock. We decided to split up and follow him for a ways. Since it was Andy's shot which wounded him, I let him follow the blood spoor, while I took out around the other side of the mountain.

The path I followed was not easy. We had left the native boys behind at the truck, so I was on my own. I had to keep constant track of landmarks so I would not become lost.

God must have been in a playful mood the day He made this part of the country, for rocks as big as three-story houses were tossed across the mountain side. Some lay flat while others stood on edge, in a weird display of savage beauty.

After stumbling around this stuff for almost an hour, I stopped in the shade to rest and wipe the perspiration from my face. I reached back for my canteen, then remembered, we had left our canteens at the truck.

My watch read three P.M. I had been on the trail for three hours. Hopefully, I had listened for the sound of a shot, which would mean that Andy had closed with our quarry. The afternoon air was quiet except for a few vultures circling far overhead. This was the time of the day when sensible people were resting in the shade. I remembered from somewhere, that the Indians of our Southwest plains, sometimes carried a pebble in their mouth to help when they were out of water. I tried this, but it only seemed to make my thirst worse.

I had about given up hope of seeing my trophy, when I rounded a big boulder. There he was, less than four hundred yards away, standing in the shade of a big thorn bush. Through the four-power scope, he looked as though I could reach out and touch him with my gun barrel. Careful, so as not to disturb him, I got into a prone position.

I knew this might be the last shot I would get. I held my breath and began the slow careful squeeze which would end in a perfect shot.

Something held me up. In the back of my mind came information I had heard a long time before. Someone once told me, that old experienced bulls would sometimes try and startle a less mature bull out of the bush to divert the hunter. For a second I took my eye off the target, as I detected a slight movement to my right. There about three hundred yards away, hunched up in the protective shadow of a big rock was my bull. I looked back at the first animal. Sure enough, he was smaller than mine. While I looked, four cows, a calf, and two small bulls grazed into sight. I guess the sight of so many lovely animals hypnotized me for a moment, for when I looked back, my quarry was on the move again. The only hopeful sign was that he seemed to be traveling slower, favoring one of his hind legs.

This went on all during the hot, dry, agonizing afternoon. Travel for an hour, get close, only to have him move on out of range. My legs were beginning to feel as though they would not support my body. My breath was coming in gasps and my tongue felt like a swollen sponge. I can remember thinking, each time I stopped to rest, I can't go on any more. It was getting on towards evening, I was out of water, and I had no idea where I might be. I was allowing myself to get into a mental state which might prove dangerous. Somehow, each time when I made up my mind to stop, something would force me to my feet just one more time.

By now, I had been on the trail for almost seven hours. The sun was sinking behind the mountains and I knew it would be dark in another thirty minutes. Already it was difficult to discern objects across the valley. If my kudu was hard hit, I knew in the darkness he would be an easy prey for hyenas. If he were not badly hurt, he would be out of that area by the next morning, even if I were in the physical shape to follow, which was doubtful.

The shadows were becoming thicker, when I saw him again. He was about a hundred and fifty yards away, a dark blur in the scope, when I put the cross hairs on him and sent a 180-grain bullet from my Savage .308 crashing into his shoulder. It was tricky shooting in the shadows and I whooped like an Indian as he went down.

I stumbled over the rocks towards him, falling and barking my already battered shins on a sharp outcropping of rock. From my left came a warning hiss and I veered sharply to the side, as the ugly head of a big snake reared threateningly over a rock. I was almost to the dark shape, when it scrambled to its feet and disappeared in the darkness. I was ready to sit beside the trail and cry like a baby.

Then my exhaustion turned to anger and I hurled myself at the ridge. Maybe, just maybe, I might get another shot at him before he disappeared. Looking into the gathering darkness below, I saw him. He was backed under a thorn bush less than thirty-five yards away. As he turned his head, I fired again and he fell for the last time, rolling down the steep slope. As I looked at this magnificent animal, I felt a pang of conscience for having caused him pain.

My problems were not over. Tired as I was, I had to do something with the animal; get help if possible before the hyenas gathered. I did not envy spending the night alone with the animal, with hungry hyenas around, epecially when I remembered I had left my matches behind at the truck. This was another case of stupidity which might have been fatal. It was the last time I was ever to leave the truck without a canteen on my belt and matches in my pocket. I guess people learn by making mistakes. Hunting rabbits or squirrels it doesn't make too much difference, but in the African bush, one such mistake can be the last.

While I was trying to decide what to do, I looked towards the west and saw the headlights of a car against the darkening sky. They were not far distant either. I hurried on a stumbling run towards the road. I couldn't afford to let them pass me. The lights came closer then stopped. I could hear the sound of the truck motor; then that stopped. Holding the muzzle of my gun in the air, I fired the two remaining shots in the magazine and was heartened when answering shots came back. I stumbled out of the brush, scratched from head to foot, my clothing torn by the rocks and thorns, tired, dirty, ready to drop from exhaustion, but triumphant.

When the truck drove up, I expected to drop, but was surprised to find myself standing straighter and feeling younger than I had in years. As I helped myself to the coolest, sweetest drink I'd ever had, Andy gave me the finest compliment I've ever received from a hunting companion:

"Jack, old man. I'll have to give you credit. I'd never expected an old man like you to make it."

We were happy to find we could drive the truck within a few yards of the animal. Andy had heard my shot more than an hour before and had headed back to the truck and come looking for me. He had seen two large bulls that afternoon, but none as large as the one which lay before us.

Within an hour, the bull was dressed out and we started the difficult job of loading him in back of the truck. Even dressed, he must have weighed close to seven hundred pounds. When we got his head and front shoulders into the truck, his rear end would slip out. When we got his rear end in, the head would not fit. Finally with two of us getting under the carcass, we managed to wrestle in into the truck.

I can still remember how filthy I was, covered with the dust and grime of ten hours on the trail, my face was streaked with dust and perspiration, my clothing was torn and blood stained. When we reached camp, I staggered out of the truck, crawled into my sleeping bag without supper and was soon dead to the world.

During the night, a hyena had invaded our camp for a bite of kudu meat. Andy fired at it, but I didn't remember anything until the next morning, when the delicious aroma of coffee and a gentle hand on my shoulder turned out to be Mohammed with a steaming cup of coffee.

The kudu was too big to put into our icebox and as we wanted to take it back whole, we decided to head back to Cheren where we could store it in a local freezer. We dropped the animal off and went west of Cheren an hour's drive, to pick up a few guinea fowl. Late Sunday afternoon, we got back to the icehouse. There was a large crowd gathered to look over the animal and everyone was exclaiming over his huge size. With some local help we got him loaded and started back towards Asmara.

At the check point just outside Cheren, we ran into our first trouble. The game official was sure he had caught a couple of game violators red handed, though why we would have driven through his check point with an illegal kudu on top of the truck was more than I could understand. Even when I showed him the permit with the chief executive's signature, he would not believe me. Only when I got the Cheren police chief to vouch for me would he let us pass.

When we reached the final check point outside Asmara, another large crowd of people was gathered. Many of them were Eritrean game officials whom I knew. The head man asked for my permit, even though he had given it to me only a few days before. He shook his head over it for some time, then held a long conference with some of his subordinates. Finally he insisted that we go with him to the police station.

By now, we were beginning to get mighty fed up. We refused, stating that we would go to the provost marshal's office first, then if he wanted us, we would go to the police. We were under special status with the Ethiopian Government and they did not have the authority to arrest us. What might have happened then I don't know, but I noticed a car drive up and recognized the driver. It was Ato Soqar Berhe, the chief prosecutor of Eritrea and my landlord. Fortunately we were good friends and my rent was paid. He came to my aid and we made our way to Kagnew Station.

At the provost marshal's office, we finally found out what had happened. When we had unloaded the kudu in Cheren, we had thrown the official Eritrean game apparatus completely out of whack. They had seen us come into Cheren with a kudu. Then we left without it. The next day, we left again with a kudu. Putting two and two together they came up with five and decided we had shot two kudus and had disposed of one in Cheren. Knowing how the official Eritrean mind works, we finally convinced them we had only shot one animal. If we had gone to the police station, there is no telling how long we would have been held there before American officials had been notified.

My kudu measured fifty-eight and a half inches around the more than three and a half spirals of his horns. He was the largest kudu shot in Ethiopia from 1950 to 1962. He was so large, that we served a dinner for 375 people at the club, with plenty of meat left over. The meat was as fine as any Kansas City beef—tender, dark red, with no wild taste. The only complaint came from one fellow who bit into a slug and lost a filling.

In 1960, I obtained another permit from the chief executive to hunt for Nubian ibex. These animals dwell on the precipitous cliffs and mountain crags at high elevations. They have an acute sense of sight and hearing and are much like the Dahl sheep of Alaska and British Columbia. At the slightest sign of danger, a shrill whistle sends them scurrying to safety and they can leap down a forty-foot precipice to a narrow ledge below.

The ibex is a typical bearded goat with enormous horns which may measure close to sixty inches in length. They rise close together from the animal's skull and sweep back in a wide, even arc like the blades of a scimitar. The horns are heavily corrugated. On a seven-day hunt, I saw two billys which would have put me in the record book for sure, but I never got closer than 800 yards to them. Very few of these animals have ever been killed by white hunters.

11 Life at an African Water Hole

Probably the most interesting sights on a safari are those seen around the water holes. This is especially true if you are hunting in arid or semi-arid country. For here you will find congregated most of the wild life of an area. If you spend enough time by one, you will see many dramas of life and death.

The most interesting water hole I can remember was on the Baraka River in northwestern Eritrea. It was located seventy miles from the closest village and was in a wilderness inhabited by wild animals and nomad tribes, who used it as their water supply.

Water is a necessity for life and in arid regions it becomes doubly precious. For a few weeks after the rainy season, no one worries about water, as it can be found in the riverbed and in many inland pot holes. During this season, it is not very profitable to hunt near the holes, for there are too many places where the animals can quench their thirst.

As the dry season progresses, usually about the end of April, these holes dry up one by one, until only the deepest of the river holes remain. Occasionally you will find holes which are fed by underground springs; these are of the utmost value and in desert country become oases.

In many cases, as the dry season progresses, man makes his own water hole by burrowing into the river bottom. Usually he can find water at first by digging only a few feet into the sand. As the dry spell progresses, however, he must dig deeper and deeper as the water level drops, until sometimes these wells reach amazing depths. Many times this project is taken on by several nomad villages, who band together to help in the community project. Often this may be the only water available for a radius of seventy miles or more and will supply hundreds of people and thousands of head of livestock.

In the summer of 1960, the great well on the Baraka River reached a depth of nearly 200 feet. As the initial hole becomes deeper and deeper, it must be shored up with palm logs. At intervals of thirty or forty feet, terraces are built which are reached by homemade ladders fastened together with vines. When the well reaches a great depth, it will usually be very narrow at the bottom, possibly only wide enough for one man to work, and flares out at the top until it looks like the diggings of some mine.

Because of the depth and these terraces, drawing water becomes a community project, with several men involved. At the lowest level, one or two men fill the goatskin water bags which are lowered on fiber ropes. These ropes are homemade from the fibers of a plant which grows in this area. Two men work on each terrace level to aid in raising the waterbags. It is obvious that much of the native's time is spent at a water hole when one observes that as many as 1,000 camel, 8000 cattle, and 50,000 goats may drink here each day, not to consider several hundred people.

During the early afternoon hours, water is drawn for

use at the villages, which may be from one-half to a mile from the well. Several tribes will often camp in the general vicinity of the well, but each will have an assigned sector for their huge herds of livestock. Each herd will have a special watering period. I never saw any mixup, or any evidence of hard feelings between the various herdsmen. It wasn't at all unusual for them to draw water for an itinerant trader on camel back and I never saw them accept pay for this rather tedious chore.

The water drawing for village use is done by the young, unmarried girls, usually those in their early teens. They come to the wells with their donkeys, each beast carrying two goatskin water bags slung on either side of a crude saddle-like affair. A water bag is attached to the rope and lowered to the bottom of the well. There the man working at water level fills it with from five to eight gallons of slightly sandy water. It is drawn progressively higher, from one terrace level to another, until it reaches the top. Sometimes there will be as many as fifty donkeys at a watering place at one time.

To get enough water for a village of five hundred people is quite a chore, so this water is used only for cooking and drinking. There is very little bathing done during the dry season. This is not because the natives are naturally dirty, for they will bathe every day during the rainy season, but because of the difficulty of obtaining water. They also use little water for washing clothes, as they believe washing wears out the clothes. I have seen many groups bathing during the rainy season when water is in abundance. They carefully undress at the edge of the pool, scrub thoroughly with sand to clean their bodies, then don the dirty clothes. Some of these clothes have not been washed in years and in a hot, goatskin tent with little ventilation, the atmosphere becomes mighty heavy. What a country for a deodorant manufacturer to settle in.

The girls work naked from the waist up and most of the native women seem to be fully developed by the age of thirteen. We used to see some real beauties, many with light golden skin and lovely features. Most nomad tribes have a very high set of moral standards and woe betide the outsider who meddles with their women. There have been instances of reluctant eunuchs being made overnight, for tampering with these desert beauties.

After the girls have finished with their water chores, the younger boys drive the herds of animals to the water. Usually goats will come first, then the long-horned cattle, and finally the camels.

A round watering trough is built from dried mud, near the opening of the well. This trough may be twenty feet in diameter and two feet deep. The sides are made from mud, which is allowed to dry in the sun until it reaches the consistency of crude cement. It crumbles easily, so care must be taken when using it. It takes a good many gallons of water to fill one of these troughs. A camel normally uses up to eight gallons of water daily, cattle from three to five, and I don't know how many goats use. This adds up to a tremendous amount of drawing, at five gallons a draw.

When the watering is finished, usually just before dark, the water trough contains about five or six inches of water. Often the natives will try and protect this trough with a wall of thorn bushes which is erected for the night. Their main enemy is the wart hog, which loves to wallow in the trough and will usually break down the sides.

As a result, most natives are happy when hunters come into their area. I have never received anything but cooperation from these nomad people and they were always glad to see us. Of course this may have been due to the fact that I gave them free medical treatment and handed out pounds of salt which in this part of Africa is almost worth its weight in gold. The natives knew we were there to cut down on the wart-hog population and this pleased them. Then, too, it gave them a chance for fresh meat, as we never threw away any meat except that of the hyena. They would not touch pork, being good Moslems, but loved gazelle meat.

A hunting blind is usually built near a water hole and depends on the prevailing winds. I have made them, using natural camouflage of bushes along the river bank. This position is not preferred for two reasons: first, in country where there are dangerous animals such as lion and leopard it is not a good idea as these animals have been known to slip up on a hunter and attack him; second, most animals come to the waterhole from the brush which is closest to the water. It is more difficult to see them if you are on the bank and it is also easier for them to detect a hunter if they pass within a few yards of where he is hidden.

I preferred to build my blind in the riverbed, possibly thirty yards from the waterhole and use a vehicle as a base. Branches and bushes are placed around the vehicle to form camouflage. It is amazing how little camouflage is necessary to fool most animals, especially a wart hog. With the leopard, it is different. Everything must be eye perfect to fool him. I also preferred a blind which was open to the rear, as I have heard of hunters who were penned in a thorn enclosure with an enraged leopard and wanted nothing of this. With two men in a blind, you can pretty well protect yourself from any attack from the rear.

One night, this type of construction almost backfired on me. We were out looking for some good wart-hog trophies, as we wanted the tusks to make candlestick holders. Every night, there was a long procession of wart hogs to the waterhole nearby and we felt as though the big pigs were coming to water late at night. All we needed was patience to wait until they arrived.

The day had been a hot one and our blind had been built in the afternoon while the cattle were still being watered. The last of the cattle herders had left and the sun was beginning to sink behind the low ridge of hills to the west.

We were already in place, with plenty of cold water to drink. Usually we didn't smoke in these blinds, as the unusual smell was something the animals didn't understand and sometimes it would spook them. Within minutes after the herders left, the procession of birds began. First a quick flight of doves that whirred in from a nearby palm grove. Then a long, solemn procession of guinea fowl paraded out of the brush, coming in single file, like soldiers moving in formation. When they got close to the water, they would suddenly break formation, dash forward a few feet, stop, then rush for the water. Sometimes two birds would jump two or three feet into the air and come together in a flurry of bodies, like two cocks fighting, then land together to drink. This comic entertainment went on for possibly thirty minutes, until suddenly for no reason at all the whole flock of several hundred birds took panic and flew off with a frantic beating of wings and much bird discussion.

Just as it was getting difficult to see objects at a distance, the first of the wart hogs arrived. This would usually be a sow with a litter of six or eight piglets. She would come out of the brush, stop to look over the area for danger, then move forward, while the piglets dashed after her.

Before she reached the water, she would stop and look carefully around once more; then assured that it was safe, some signal must have been passed to the piglets, for they dashed squealing to wallow in the water.

The wart hog is one of the most pugnacious animals found in the bush. Its tusks are deadly weapons which it knows how to use effectively and, given a chance, it will defend itself and its young against a leopard. When it is being chased, it will back down into its burrow while at full speed, presenting a face full of tusks to the intruder. It trots around the veldt with an air of comic importance and egotism as though it were big and tough enough to take on anything in sight. It is so ugly, its looks alone should scare off most opponents.

The wart hog has the distinction of being considered the ugliest animal on earth. Its head appears to be much too large in proportion to the rest of its body. Its legs are short, the feet small. The head is as repulsive as something from a bad dream. Two pairs of grotesque warts appear on each side of a scoop-like face and the bleary piggish eyes are sunk in bags of wrinkled skin. Near the end of the snout are tusks which curl up and over and which may reach a length of twenty-seven inches. The largest I shot was twenty-one and a half. A large boar will stand thirty inches at the front shoulder and weigh close to three hundred pounds. In spite of their repulsiveness, the sows and piglets are delicious eating. The boar, especially an old one, is apt to be tough and pretty strong. The animal is a vegetarian, living on roots and tubers. It is also much like the domestic hog, in that given the opportunity it will eat meat.

As the evening progresses, the pigs coming to water become progressively larger, The big boars come in by themselves late at night and are very wary. On this night, seventy-five pigs were counted at this one hole. Sometimes it is difficult to tell just how large a pig is. One of my first times out, I almost shot at a pig who stood blinking in the light of the spotlight. I thought he had an enormous set of tusks. When I looked closer, it was nothing but long, white bristles which grew beside his snout.

It seems strange, but bright lights seldom bother these animals. We would wait until the pigs began to drink, then turn on the spotlight. The usual reaction was for them to look up a moment, then go back to their drinking.

By this time, it was getting late. We had seen some big boars, but nothing of the type we were looking for. It is a strange thing, but you cannot tell the size of the tusks by the size of the pig. In some areas, small pigs will have huge curved tusks, while in other areas, very large pigs will have small tusks. I believe it depends a good deal on the type of food they have in certain areas and maybe even on the mineral content of the ground. By eleven o'clock, we were about ready to give up and go back to camp. I sat back against the car, leaned my gun against a fender, and reached for a cigar, when I heard the sound of movement close behind me. I grabbed up a hand flashlight and turned it on. Standing less than ten feet away was one of the biggest, meanest-looking boars I had ever seen. He was clashing together as fine a set of tusks as I'd seen and at this close range I could almost feel them tear into my flesh.

As I yelled to Pat, the pig turned to run. Pat, sitting near the big light, turned it on and we were able to follow the pig's progress down the river. By this time, I had recovered enough to grab up my rifle. In the cone of light, I could see the big boar clearly in the cross-hairs of the scope. I squeezed the trigger gently, keeping the sight centered just a little ahead of the plunging black form. As the shot sounded, the big boar did a cartwheel, to land silent in the sand. It was one of the finest running shots I had ever made and considering that it was done by artificial light, I felt pretty proud. To be honest with you, it just had to be one of those lucky shots. The tusks of the boar measured a bit more than eighteen inches.

Gazelle seldom drink from a water hole, although they often hang around the vicinity of one. These amazing little creatures seem to get enough moisture from dew-laden grass to take care of their needs, even in desert areas. One night, sitting at a water hole, we heard a strange sound behind us. It sounded rather like two men fighting with sticks, beating them together as they parried blows. When we turned on the light, it was two big Grant's gazelle bucks locked in furious combat. We watched them for at least ten minutes before they stopped and trotted off into the bush. I often wished my camera equipment had been such that I could take night pictures, for there are many dramas which take place then that are not seen at any other time.

Many other animals can be seen around a water hole, often depending on the areas in which you are located. In Kenya for instance, one animal seen in large numbers is the wildebeeste, sometimes called the gnu. This animal, which is part of the antelope family, gives the impression of having been put together from parts of other animals. It seems to have the body of a cow, the legs of a gazelle, the mane and tail of a horse. It is a nervous animal which always seems to be kicking, biting and bucking, for no apparent reason than to be just raising cain.

Sometimes other smaller, nocturnal animals will be seen, either at the water hole, or on the journey there. Animals like the elephant shrew, which is no larger than a rat. Its chubby, soft-furred body ends in long rear legs and it hops around for all the world like a miniature kangaroo It has very large eyes. Sometimes you will see two of them standing on their hind legs and using their front feet like boxers.

The springhaus or jumping hare is also an unusual member of the smaller animals. It is sandy colored, about a foot tall when sitting on it's haunches. It has a long tail, with a brush at its end. For some reason this little creature is attracted to camps and you can often sit around the campfire and see the flames reflected in its eyes. It moves like a kangaroo, taking two-foot leaps. It lives in complicated burrows in the ground which may cover a hundred yards and have six or eight openings. It is said to sleep sitting on its haunches and never comes out during daylight. When it goes into the burrow, it closes the opening with an earthen plug.

Another animal seen frequently at a water hole is the common dog of Africa, the jackal. In some places in Africa, this little fellow is called the "lion's provider." It usually hunts in groups of three to six and can run for speeds of up to thirty-five miles per hour for a considerable length of time. You often hear these animals at night. They sound similar to our coyote: a long wail that is repeated several times in succession, each pitched slightly higher until it ends in a sharp yelp.

Probably one of the most hated and feared animals in Africa is the African hunting dog. These terrible animals hunt in packs of up to sixty animals and will run down and kill even the big antelopes. When a pack arrives in an area, most of the animals promptly move out. Sometimes they will risk being caught by a crocodile and will swim a stream to get away from the dogs. They are very similar to our

North American wolf, about four feet long, with long legs, a big head, powerful jaws, and a long bushy tail. They are tortoise shell color, with blotches of yellow, black, and white and are sometimes called "hyena dogs."

One of the interesting burrowing animals found in most of East Africa is the aardvark. This is a large, donkey-eared animal. It has a long, pointed snout, a fat, round body with scant brown or gray hair. It looks so much like a pig, early Dutch settlers named it by putting together two Dutch words, "aard" for "earth," and "vark" for "pig." Its legs are short and thick, with four toes on the front feet and five on the rear. It may reach a length of four feet and weigh up to a hundred pounds.

The natives love its meat and will crawl down into its burrow armed with a knife. When the kill is made, they tap on the roof of the tunnel and his companions sink a vertical tunnel to the game. The flesh and teeth are also used to make charms which are said to ward off ill fortune.

Another peculiar animal found throughout East Africa is the scaly anteater. When it is rolled into a ball, it resembles a huge pine cone. Its back and sides seem to be made of linked armor, as it is covered from head to tail with large, overlapping, pointed scales. These scales are horny in texture and sharp on the outer edge. It is a master at self-defense, for when attacked, it will roll into a tight ball and erect its sharp scales, presenting armor with knife-like blades which bristle at the enemy. When disturbed it makes a loud hissing sound and will slash with its tail with unexpected speed and power, driving the sharp blades deep into the flesh of its foe. It has no teeth, as it lives on ants and termites. Its head is small, its face pointed, with a long, sticky tongue which picks up the insects. With its sharp, strong claws, it rips open the termite nests. It protects its young by rolling them into the center of its body. The largest of these animals is found in Equatorial Africa where they reach a length of six feet, with scales five inches by three inches in size. It lives in ground burrows. This animal is very strong. Two men cannot unroll it by hand while it is still alive. The scales are so tough, they will turn a .30 rifle bullet fired at a hundred yards. The scales of this animal are also used for charms and are believed by the natives to possess supernatural power.

Sometimes also, the water hole will be visited by such nocturnal animals as the hyena and cheetah. One unforgettable night, we counted twenty-eight of the beautiful hunting cats as they came to refresh themselves at our stand.

The water hole is to Africa what the soda fountain is to American teenagers.

12   Home of the Gods

Many people think of Africa as a land of jungles. It has these—vast areas which stretch into the unknown and some never having been seen by white man. Still the vastness of Africa is not made up of jungles. In the north, from Egypt and the Red Sea to Morocco and the Atlantic Ocean, vast oceans of sand dominate the landscape. There are places of great fertility within this area, such as the Nile Delta country and some of the larger oases within the desert itself, but one never has to go far to find the sand.

The great majority of the rest of the country is made up of veldt country and mountain ranges. Most of the veldt, or bush country, is at fairly high altitudes. There are huge plateaus in East Africa which stretch for hundreds of miles. Because of this predominately high altitude, East Africa is not the steaming hot place many people think it is. There are areas here which will vie for record with the hottest places in the world. Massawa, on the Red Sea, has the reputation of being the hottest seaport in the world and I have seen the summer temperature hit 156 degrees here and never drop below 100 at night for six weeks at a time.

Most of the plains areas have temperatures which are

better than those of our plains states. Days are often hot under the tropical sun, but evenings become so cool that sweaters and fires are welcome. There is usually little humidity, so the heat is not ennervating.

Someone has called East Africa the "home of the gods." This is probably because of the native superstition that their gods live in the high mountains. One has only to see the majestic, snow-covered peak of Kilimanjaro or Kenya to understand why the superstitious natives feel this way. I can think of no more suitable place for mortal gods to dwell than on these magnificent mountains. They possess all the qualifications of a Mt. Olympus.

In the new republic of Tanzania, better known as Tanganyika, the home of the local gods is on Mt. Kilimanjaro, the highest peak in Africa and one of the highest in the world. The gods of Kilimanjaro are bashful and you can only see their home on rare occasions, when the mists rise for a few minutes, to reveal the mountain in all its snow-covered glory.

When the mists do rise for a few moments, Kilimanjaro is one of the most beautiful mountains in the world rivalling the great volcano in Japan, Mt. Fujiyama. It towers to the imposing height of 19,720 feet and although it is only a few miles south of the equator, its top is always covered with snow and ice glaciers. This phenomenon can be seen in all three East African countries: Tanzania has Kilimanjaro, Kenya its Mt. Kenya, and Uganda the Ruwenzori's (Mountains of the Moon).

A journey to the top of Kilimanjaro is like a journey in miniature from the equator to the Arctic. From the banana groves at the foot of the mountain, one passes through thick, tropical rain forests, then through various belts of vegetation until reaching the eternal snows.

Kilimanjaro is actually composed of two peaks: The tallest is Mt. Kibo, while Mt. Mawenzi is a jagged peak that rises some 17,000 feet above sea level, about the same as Mt. Kenya farther to the north.

Most visitors approach Kilimanjaro from the north and pass through the Amboseli Game Preserve, one of the largest game sanctuaries in East Africa. An amazing number of animals can be seen here.

Leaving the Mombasa-Nairobi railroad at Kibwezi, we motored south in a Land Rover which had been converted into a comfortable bus. This did nothing to halt the dense clouds of dust, though, which in my opinion are the worst hazard of motor travel in Africa.

When we asked the guide where Lake Amboseli was, he said we were traveling through it at the time. About the only water which can be seen is in the beautiful blue mirages, complete with palm trees which one sees in the distance.

Driving along over the white surface of the waterless lake, which glared in the sun as much as if there had been water, we saw several hyenas shambling along after a small herd of gazelle. They all appeared to be lame, but this is only a hyena characteristic and is due to the peculiar conformation of their body.

Once you reach the neighborhood of Lake Amboseli, the game begins to thicken. Herds of a hundred or more zebra are not unusual, while wildebeeste buck and show off for the visitor, running around as though they were crazy.

Gazelles will be over the vast area in such numbers, that soon you will hardly pay any attention to these lovely ceratures. I was fascinated by the giraffes. Two big fellows were eating out of the top of a thorn bush which must have been all of twelve-foot tall. I guess all giraffes eat from the top of trees and bushes, but when you look at the length of their bodies, it would be quite a chore to bend down to eat grass. When they drink, they get down to water level by spreading their front legs apart at an almost impossible angle. One young fellow was seen peeking out from behind the protection of his mother, with his neck outstretched and eyes almost popping from his head, as he looked at these peculiar creatures who were invading his home.

Not too far off the road, a big female elephant came out of the bush, to stand with cabbage ears opened like some type of hearing aid. Her trunk was stretched toward us and it looked as though she was ready to charge. Then we saw the reason for her nervousness, as the bushes parted and a little "toto" came out to stand beside the bulk of his mother. She forgot us for the moment and stopped to fondle junior, telling him that everything was okay and that mama would look out for him.

Farther along, a big bull was wrestling with a stubborn tree limb, with all four feet braced. He had his trunk wrapped around the limb and was pulling and grunting for all he was worth. Other trees in the neighborhood showed there were other elephants about, for bits of chewed fiber lay around on the ground. Elephants eat trees in the same way that natives eat sugar cane.

As we approached Kilimanjaro, we began to see rhino and buffalo. There are many swamps in this area and the big rhinos love to wallow in the water like pigs. One evening we stayed in a little tourist camp—I can't remember its name—where the huts were built on the principle of the native rondavel. We went to sleep to the sleepy clucking of a flock of guinea fowl who were roosting in the branches overhead. During the night, I was awakened by a sound which made me think a steam engine had stopped outside our door. I knew there were no railroad tracks close by.

Going to the window, I could see the massive bulk of a big rhino standing outside the door. I was certainly glad he was only passing through.

The vast Amboseli Preserve stretches for mile on dusty mile, through the brush country and into the home land of those, "bravest of the brave," the Masai tribe. The Masai are noted fighters. Before they can become full-fledged "morans" (warriors), they must kill a lion in single combat, armed with a spear.

When it comes time for a young warrior to be initiated into this warrior clan, he will go out with other full-fledged warriors, until they find a pride of lions. They close with a lion and attempt to make it charge. Often the warrior will rush towards the big cat, then kneel and shake his shield in a taunting manner. Finally when the lion can stand it no more, he will come for the youth in a roaring charge. When the lion is twenty feet away (one good leap), the neophyte will throw his spear. Sometimes he does this with such force it passes completely through the charging animal. He then doubles up under the protection of his shield, while the other morans close with the beast and spear it to death. The man behind the shield is usually badly clawed and bitten, but he wears these scars as a mark of honor, much like old-time Prussians wore scars from saber duels.

When fighting a man, the lion usually stands up on its hind legs, like the animal on a coat of arms and will spar and box with its front paws like a boxer. The only difference being that each blow is strong enough to break the neck of a bull. In addition, he has a fist full of needle-sharp claws and a dew-claw on each foreleg. These claws are about two inches long and are something like a man's thumb. They are curved and very sharp. Usually you do not see these claws for they are kept folded against the lion's leg. He can extend them like a brush hook and striking with them can disembowel a man with one slash.

A friend of mine saw one of these initiation ceremonies. He told me the bravest thing a moran can do is to grab the tail of the charging lion near its root and hang on while his comrades slash the lion to bits with their spears and simis. "At times like these," he said, "the warriors work themselves into such a frenzy, they do not feel the pain from wounds which have been inflicted." Most of them exhibit deep scars with a great deal of pride.

The Masai spears are of interest, in that they are made of bits of iron which are found in stream beds. The native smiths do not understand fully how to temper this metal and the spear points are usually soft. It is no trouble for a man to bend one over his knee. The blades of these spears are narrow and some four feet long. If they strike the bone of an animal, they will bend at 45-degree angle.

When throwing the spear, the moran takes up a position similar to that used by a target shooter, with his left foot slightly advanced for balance. The whole weight of his body is behind the cast and the flight of the spear through the air is so rapid it actually whistles. Many of the spears have ridges on the sides which cause the spear to rotate and adds to the accuracy. The warriors are unbelievably accurate with these weapons up to seventy-five feet and can hit a moving target with little trouble.

At one time the Masai were the most feared warriors in this part of Africa. Now they have become herdsmen. During the Mau Mau trouble, the chiefs offered the British a force of 3,000 spearmen to fight against the bandits, but the British wisely turned them down. It has been a hard job to get them to their present semi-civilized state.

The hunting areas near Mt. Kenya are not as good as those near Kilimanjaro, as civilization has made many inroads in this area and some of the finest resort hotels in East Africa are found on the lower slopes of this mountain. However, one of the most primitive areas in Africa is still found on one of its slopes. This is the Abadare Forest, which was one of the prime hangout areas of the Mau Mau.

To the west, in Uganda, there are many wonderful hunting areas. Millions of animals may be seen on the vast Queen Elizabeth Preserve. Hunting in Uganda and northwestern Tanzania is among the best left in the world. Here you can still see vast herds of zebra, gazelle, wildebeeste, hartbeeste, impala, topi, and other varieties, running together with a few prides of lion hanging on close to the outskirts.

There is one vast area in Africa that has been barely scratched by the white hunter. This is in central Sudan, centering around the city of Juba. Due to political upheavals, red tape, and the difficulty of reaching this area, few white men have hunted here. Now this area is being opened up to hunters and offers some of the old-time hunting thrills which have made Africa the mecca for big game hunters from all over the world. Safaris from Nairobi are now offered into southern Sudan, although due to the distance which must be traveled, they are quite expensive.

13 Sudanese Adventure

"We've finally made it, Jack," he said. There was a touch of emotion in his voice which in itself was unusual. "We've finally made it, after sweating it out for four damn years." The speaker was big Earlin Wilson, better known to his friends as "Big Willy."

We were seated on a canvas cot in the shade of an enormous thorn tree which must have covered half an acre in its shade. The sun was sinking in a red fireball behind a fringe of stately palm trees which lined the river bank. It was our first day in a hunting camp in central Sudan. We had dreamed and planned for this trip for three years.

This country held me spellbound. Not that I hadn't seen strange country before. I had spent four tours of duty in the Far East and one in North Africa. I had traveled all over Europe and East Africa during the four years I had been at Kagnew Station. What really stirred me now was to think that the little country boy who had spent so many hours daydreaming about this same country was now sitting under a tree in its very center. I couldn't remember how many math and English classes I had sat through in a daze while my mind was thousands of miles away, but from the looks of some of my report cards, it must have been many.

Now, many years later, here I was, sitting in the heart of a virgin hunting paradise.

For fourteen hours, since the cold, gray of an African morning had broken, we had been making our slow, jolting, and often painful way across the vast Sudanese plains. In all those dusty miles covered, we had seen no sign of human habitation, save for a few lonely herdsmen and even these had become scarce as the late afternoon sun blazed down.

The country had been changing throughout the day. When we started that morning, the countryside was made up of rough lava rocks. A small mountain range bordered the trail. Now we were in the center of a vast plain, which was covered with eight-foot elephant grass.

There was nothing to break the monotony of this brown, saw-toothed grass, except an occassional thorn bush shading a herd of sleepy gazelle, or a flock of guinea fowl who cursed us for disturbing their afternoon siesta. Once a long-legged ostrich crossed our track, moving in vast disdain. Later we were treated to a fleeting glimpse of a beautiful sable antelope, as he crossed a clearing ahead of us in a dazzling burst of speed, his magnificent scimitar-shaped horns laid back against his rump as he ran.

Outside of this, here had been nothing but the heat and the everlasting dust which rose in stifling clouds. A few vultures circled lazily overhead in the brassy sky. Hordes of sticky, aggressive flies descended on us every time we stopped. Nothing seemed to keep the pesky insects from bothering us. Our modern insect repellents seemed to be like nectar to them and all we could do was cover our exposed skin and literally "sweat it out" under the blazing sun. How we envied the native boys, who could sleep with flies crawling over their faces. It bothered them not a bit.

This trip was the result of four years of careful planning. For some time, I had been associated with a group of dedicated hunters—men who like myself loved the outdoors. We were interested in hunting, not only from the shooting angle, but also from the conservation angle. Each of us had a great love for the marvelous things God had placed in this world for the happiness of man. A hunting trip was not a license for us to kill, for all of us had passed up many opportunities to shoot trophy-size animals because we already had better trophies. It had become an unwritten law in our group, that we would only kill for camp meat, or for a trophy we did not have. Other than that, our field trips were for the pure joy of being in the great unknown and in enjoying our good fellowship. Our field trips were not to get away from our families, or to indulge in drunken brawls; we liked each other's company and came away from one of these trips feeling that we knew both God and our fellow man better.

Game like hyena, baboon, and some of the other pests was a different thing altogether, although I could not bring myself to kill baboon just for the fun of it.

We had made numerous inquiries about a trip into the central part of that huge area which makes up the country of Sudan. Most of the information we received was discouraging. In 1960, Willy and I had made a brief trip across the border of western Ethiopia, but it was only through the good offices of a local Sudanese official. Now, we were out to enter that country and travel thousands of miles in its interior.

In 1961, a lieutenant colonel was assigned to Kagnew Station, who was to have a great effect on the hunting policies of Kagnew Station. He was the new judge advocate. His assignment was of special interest to me, for I had served with Cass in pre-war Korea and we were good friends. I had introduced him to the lovely lady who finally became Mrs. Beimfohr.

The colonel was an old African hand and had been on safari in Kenya during the Mau Mau rebellion in 1954. From experience gained in military advisory duty, the colonel had become a firm believer in the efficacy of personal contacts. One of his first efforts along this line was to meet the local Sudanese consul in Asmara. Not only did he succeed in meeting this man, he also became a personal friend of his. This fine gentleman was to be our official contact with the Sudanese Government in Khartoum. Eventually, he was to obtain the necessary permits and visas for an extended stay in his country.

Almost a year elapsed from the time our request for hunting permits had gone to Khartoum, until we received word they had been approved. We were further elated to find that our long wait had been worthwhile, for the consul had somehow managed to get resident licenses for us. This was a tremendous savings over fees charged to other big game hunters.

Our licenses, which were Class "C," covered the taking of twenty-seven different types of game, with a total of forty-seven animals allowed. The cost was $17.00 U.S. currency for a thirty-day hunt. Rhino were strictly protected, but we could shoot elephant on payment of a daily fee of two pounds, about $5.60. Our permits covered the taking of cape buffalo, lion, leopard, roan antelope, sable, tiang, bush buck, reed buck, wild pig, greater and lesser kudu, and a large variety of smaller gazelle and antelope.

This was to be a trial trip for U.S. military personnel. We set out to accomplish two definite objectives. The first was

to create a feeling of goodwill between the officials and natives of the hunting area and Americans, through our personal actions; the second was to see just how economically
this trip could be made. There were many military personnel in Asmara who would jump at the opportunity to go
to Sudan, but they could not afford a large cash outlay.

Five men were invited to make the trip: Col. Cass Beimfohr, Big Willy, Harv Barrows, and a big blonde fellow from
East Peoria, Illinois, by the name of Jim Fox. I was the fifth
member of the party.

Our entourage was kept to a minimum. We were sure
we could supplement our camp help from local sources.
Two good men were taken along. One was Abraham, an
Eritrean who spoke Sudanese. He was an expert skinner.
Our other regular was Fadul, the cook. Fadul was inval-
uable to us because he was a Sudanese national and could
speak the language fluently. He was also Moslem, a belief
which coincided with that held by most of the Sudanese
natives.

As we were planning the trip, I wondered how five men
could make a trip of this type for the $1,000 we had allotted.
I had seen several fashionable safaris leave Nairobi. They
were going on a thirty-day trip for two and the tab was in
the neighborhood of $5,000.

Space was a prime factor in our planning. We were to
be miles from civilization during much of our trip and had
to carry all the necessities of life. Corner service stations and
groceries were few and far between. Our trip was planned
around the transportation available. The basis of this was
two Land Rovers and the Dodge power wagon we were to
rent from Special Services for $2 per day. The truck would
haul a trailer and there would be another trailer which
would be hauled alternately by the hunting cars.

Fuel is costly in Sudan, running from 65c to 75c per gallon. We hoped to take along enough of the 18c fuel we could purchase at Kagnew Station to last the whole trip. This would compose the greatest part of our load. The one bright spot was that our load would become lighter with each mile we traveled. The 55-gallon gasoline drums would not be excess weight, for we had heard they were valuable in trade with the natives.

Our trip had been planned for the dry season, so we could keep our camping equipment to a minimum. We did not take tents. A large tarpaulin was taken to cover the equipment in the truck. It could also be used if we ran into an unexpected shower. The rest of the load was made up of folding cots, mosquito nets, sleeping bags, food, cooking utensils, and water. Our initial water supply came from ten, five-gallon cans. This was replenished from local sources as we went along and was purified by the use of chlorine tablets.

Most of the food stock was in canned goods, which we hoped to supplement with fresh foods procured locally and with meat from the animals we shot. We had been warned the Sudanese were great tea drinkers, a habit they no doubt acquired from the British; so we took along a plentiful supply of tea. For the American coffee drinkers, there was plenty of the ground bean.

We were pleased to find we could trade for many of the fresh food stuffs needed. Most of the natives we encountered had little use for money, but were anxious to get such supplies as salt. We brought along 200 kg (about 450 lbs) to use in curing our trophies. On one occasion, we had ostrich eggs for breakfast. These huge eggs made an omelet comparable to that made from two dozen eggs. It was delicious.

This chapter is a resumé of our trip, taken from my daily diary:

February 2, 1962: After sweating out our official papers for two years, they finally arrived today and we started loading. Our initial gasoline supply will be carried in 10—55 gallon drums which we hope will last the trip. This is in addition to 110 gallons carried in the vehicles. The fuel itself is a good deal of weight, some 5200 pounds. I don't know how the old truck will stand up under the pounding it will take on the rough Sudanese roads, for it is loaded now until the springs are down on the axles. The two trailers are almost as bad. Fortunately we have plenty of good tires, with three spares for the truck and two each for the Rovers. Of course we are taking along a tire repair kit.

February 3, 1962: Everything is ready to go. This morning, Willy and I went down to Zacherelli's garage (he is the local Land Rover representative) and picked up extra parts for the two hunting cars. We got a real break from Emilio, which more than justifies my argument that it pays to treat people with consideration. Unfortunately some of our American people like to impress the locals by acting like big shots. I've never gone along with this. Long ago I came to the conclusion that the golden rule is a mighty good thing to live by. I've found that it pays in the long run to treat people with respect and dignity, whether they are educated, or natives from the bush. Fortunately, I was a good friend of Emilio and drove a car he sponsored in local auto races. We trusted each other. He gave us a large stock of new parts for the Land Rovers, with the agreement that we would pay for what we used when we got back.

The original safari kitty started out with $350. This was in addition to the $17 apiece we spent for our licenses. The colonel will pick up the final paper work from the consul this afternoon and if all goes according to plan, we will be off early Sunday morning.

February 4, 1962: Got up at four-thirty this morning. Could have been ready at three, as I didn't sleep well at all last night. Was too excited about the trip. Much like I used to be as a boy when dad took me on a fishing trip. Harv picked me up at the BEQ at five and we stopped at the Kagnew Station guard house, where we will meet the rest of the gang. John Houseworth, one of the MP's, had a pot of coffee on and it sure tasted good. It's mighty chilly this time of the morning, about like October weather back in North Dakota. We signed out as per regulations and were about to leave when Harv discovered he had left all his papers at home and had to go back after them. This is the first delay of the trip.

Finally got underway at six-fifteen. We followed the paved road north through Cheren—this made my sixty-eighth trip over this section of the road—then hit a pretty good gravel road at the 125 km marker. This road took us to the border at Tessenai. The weather started out pretty chilly and gloves and jackets felt good. Now it is 8:30, we are just entering Cheren and the sun is warm enough so we can strip off the outergarments.

Stopped at the hotel for a bite to eat, then left at nine on the next lap of the trip through Agordat and Barentu. Hope that guard isn't on the check point at Agordat or we may be held up there. He's been on duty three times in the last couple of months and every time he's caused us trouble. It's a beautiful day, with just a hint of coolness in the air now. We're rolling along at a brisk 45 mph. About two o'clock, just as we were leaving Barentu, the tail pipe on my Land Rover came loose, caught in one of the rear tires and tore off most of the tread. Who would have thought the newest vehicle would be the one to give us the first trouble? Trouble sure does come from unexpected sources.

Cass and I changed tires. When we finally caught up with Willy and the truck, they were pulled over beside the road changing a flat. Both of the truck spares are low on air, something we evidently failed to check before leaving Asmara. Wonder what else we forgot? Stopped at the police station at Aicota, but they had no air there. Did have a cold drink and a short conversation with the police lieutenant. This was the first of a good many diplomatic visits we made on the trip.

We reached the outskirts of Tessenai at five. The customs office is closed on Sunday, so we'll camp here tonight and be ready for an early start tomorrow. Fadul has supper cooking and it sure smells good. Puppy just whipped a visiting native dog and sent him off with his tail between his legs. Might be a good idea to tell who Puppy is. He will play an important part in this trip. He is a big "yaller dog" owned by Willy. Don't know for sure what his pedigree is, but he looks like a cross between a Great Dane and a German Sheperd. He's built like the proverbial "out house," square and strong and will weigh close to 150 pounds. Puppy was brought along as a watch dog and will fill this position with admirable dispatch. As a diplomat he isn't so hot, for he hates all "furriners." To Puppy, all people who aren't in our hunting party are "furriners." He isn't too happy with the native boys. Have to keep him tied at all times to avoid an international incident.

February 5, 1960: (The day the sky fell in.) Broke camp at seven and headed into Tessenai after a good breakfast. This was to be the only good thing of the whole day. It was a beautiful day until we hit the Customs Office, then it clouded up in a hurry. We had hoped to clear here in an hour, but by one o'clock, we were still locked in mortal combat with a stupid individual who was trying to show

how important he was. He was important all right, for he was holding us up. Finally got a long distance telephone call through to Asmara, where the head man assured him it was okay to let us through. He just couldn't get it through his little pointed head, that we were leaving the country for Sudan and that we expected to re-enter at this same place. He finally let us go at two, after the colonel threatened to write a complaint to the chief executive.

Traveling north from Tessenai, the country becomes a lot more rugged. The road does not climb into the mountains, but low, rugged hills border the road most of the way. Don't rightly know if they should be called hills or not. They are more like huge rock formations. The road wends its way through these rocks and the rough lava roadbed really raises cain with the tires. Reached Kassala at five and was delighted to find we could clear Sudanese customs in thirty minutes. Was much impressed with the courtesy of the officials, a pleasant contrast with that of Eritrea.

Our hunting permits still haven't reached here from Khartoum. We hope they will be here by tomorrow morning. The local game official told us they had received a wire from their headquarters stating they would arrive then.

We camped out in a pleasant grove near the Gash River. While the boys were setting up camp, the colonel and I payed a visit on the governor. We were surprised to find Kassala is a very pretty little city, setting out here as it does in the middle of desolate plains. It has a decided British touch and many of its officials speak English with a British accent. The governor's residence is a palatial home built years ago by the British and would be at home in Lancaster or Nottingham. The city has many beautiful homes and the streets are bordered with flower beds which are quite breathtaking in their color. We were told the city's water is supplied from 1,000 artesian wells. This area is noted for its truck gardening, cotton, and bananas. Bananas and cotton grown here are trans-shipped through Eritrea, through the port at Massawa, and then north to Europe. We were able to supplement our fresh food supply, even to a huge stalk of bananas.

The hour spent at the governor's mansion was most profitable. We were taken into the garden and served ice tea. After a pleasant visit, we went on our way with the promise from the governor that he would have letters made up to police chiefs and village chiefs along our route. He would request them to help us as much as possible.

The governor was the first good glimpse I got of the Sudanese people, and I was very impressed with what I saw. During the trip, I developed a real liking for these people. Discourtesy was the exception rather than the rule and we received nothing but courteous treatment from all the officials we met.

When we reached camp, we were much impressed with the progress we had made officially. Puppy is the only sour note in the whole trip so far. He doesn't care for diplomacy and has been scaring the dickens out of the natives, who are too curious and get within range. Already he has developed a cute trick. He lays in wait under the truck until someone gets in range, then sails out and nails them. One old man was a bit too curious. Luckily Puppy's rope held and all the old man lost was a bit of his dirty robe and dignity.

February 6, 1962: Had a good night's sleep, with no hyenas to bother us. The only thing that broke the serenity of the night was a herd of camels which is now down by the river; they make a sound so much like the roar of a lion, it scares the devil out of you at first. We breakfasted early and broke camp, so we would reach the governor's office by eight o'clock. We got our letters of introduction as promised. The clearances came through about 8:30. The only unpleasantness we have run into in Sudan so far has been with the bank people and then only because they are so slow. It took an hour and a half to get them to change a few American dollars into Sudanese currency.

Finally got underway at one o'clock. The day is hot and the roads are dusty and rough, but not as bad as we had expected. Local officials gave us the good word that they get worse farther south. The vehicles are operating okay, with the exception of the truck. Old "Death and Destruction," as we call her, gets a vapor lock everytime we stop and shut off the engine. Then it takes thirty minutes until she will deign to start again. Got into Gedaref about seven, to find the police chief had received a telephone call from the governor and was waiting for us. We will camp within the police compound tonite. Feels as though I'm coming down with a terrible cold; my bones ache and I feel like "death warmed over." Doesn't look as though we will spend a very pleasant night. Already the ground is beginning to freeze and the wind is blowing clouds of dust through the compound. Dinner looked and smelled good, but I just wasn't up to eating any of it. Fadul took time out to heat me a bowl of soup and I'm hitting the sack early.

February 7, 1962: Got up early this morning and ran head on into the first really unpleasant incident of the trip. The colonel left to see the police commissioner. While he was gone, some fancy dressed dude walked through our camp area and began to pry into the backs of the vehicles, lifting up the covers on the trailers. When he opened the lid on my foot locker and looked inside, I was ready to get him myself, even though I felt like the devil. Puppy did the job for me. He walked by the truck where Puppy was tied and the big dog waited patiently until he lifted the canvas on the back, then came sailing out to nail him but good. The uninvited visitor beat a hasty retreat, but not before the "yaller" dog grabbed him by the leg, tearing his pants and taking some hide with it. To our consternation, the uninvited visitor turned out to be a police lieutenant.

The officer was mad and demanded we shoot the dog at once. I was afraid all the good will we had tried to build up would dissolve with this one incident, for Willy was ready to defend the pup against all comers, including the Sudanese army if necessary.

Our troubles were solved. In the middle of an argument with the lieutenant, the colonel arrived with the police major. After listening carefully to both sides of the story, the major gave his verdict. This was spoken in English for our benefit. He spoke sternly to the angry lieutenant:

"Why did you walk through these people's camp without their permission?" he asked. "Would you like it if some stranger walked through your home like this? The dog was only doing his duty when he bit you. You had no business poking around in these people's personal belongings. What will these Americans think of us Sudanese if I let one of my officers make such an ass of himself? You should be ashamed and apologize. I am embarassed that an officer of mine is such a fool."

We left in a few minutes with the police chief's blessing for a happy and successful trip.

"I hope you will not judge all Sudanese by this ass," he said. "I only ask one favor. Please watch the dog and let me know if he gets sick." I was never sure whether his interest was for the lieutenant or for Puppy.

The roads got rougher and rougher as we went farther

south, just as they said they would. Really they are only sandy trails cross country, but they are used by huge trucks which carry cotton from the cotton plantations along the Nile River. The ruts in the sand are so deep our axles drag a lot of the time. The dust here is the consistency of flour and may be as much as two feet deep. It pushes up ahead of the tires like water before the prow of a boat. No matter how fast you travel, the dust rises in choking clouds which gets into everything, even the foot lockers. To make things even worse, a can of shaving lather exploded in my locker. You should see the mess that makes when mixed with dust. Most of the time we had to drive with handkerchiefs tied over our noses and mouths. In the heat, the perspiration and dust made mud masks which were quite grotesque.

We reached the town of Qual 'en Nahl about three and stopped for a cold Coca-Cola. We were told the ford over the river at El Hawata was impassable, so it will be necessary to detour 175 miles out of the way to cross. The bridge has been out for five years.

The detour will take us through the village of Moka. It looks like good lion country and we are tempted to stop for a few days. The local natives tell us the hunting is poor hereabouts, so we will go on. We will set up a temporary camp here on the banks of the Rahad River.

During the evening a local cattle herder came to camp. When he herd we were going hunting, he wanted to sign on as a guide. He told us the hunting a day's drive to the south was very good with buffalo, lion, and roan antelope. We found out later, the area he was talking about was in the middle of a game preserve.

This old fellow looked for all the world like an Old Testament character with his scraggly beard and flowing robes. He wanted twenty pounds, about $56, for thirty days of work. I'm sure he would have been disappointed if we had taken him up on this offer, as most Sudanese like to dicker. We finally settled on him for eight pounds (about $20). We were to furnish his food and tobacco. In the end the old boy got the best of the bargain, as he was the laziest individual I've ever seen and he chain smoked his way through three or four packs of cigarettes a day. We finally rationed him to one pack per day, over his screams, which could be heard a mile away. He also was a tea drinker, but did not use sugar in his tea. Instead he dampened his sugar with the tea and I believe I'd be well within the bounds of truthfulness if I said he used half a cup of sugar with each cup of tea. He was the only sour note we struck on the whole trip as far as the natives were concerned and we were stuck with him. Because of his original salary demand, we nicknamed him "Old Twenty Pounds." His real name was Nur El Bey.

February 8, 1962: The night was bitter even though we are only at 2500 feet elevation. There was frost on the ground and ice formed on the edges of the river. Who would think we are only 10 degrees north of the equator? After a good breakfast with fresh eggs from the village, we got underway with "Old Twenty Pounds" riding in the power wagon. He complained bitterly because we wouldn't let him ride in state in the back of the Land Rover. Already he is pouting like a little boy and I doubt if we will get very much good from him. He's an expert on everything, but does work on nothing.

To make it easier on everyone, we are taking turns driving. "Old Death and Destruction" really takes a lot out of a man on these roads and in this heat.

Our first mechanical trouble hit us about an hour after we got started. One of the overload springs on the truck broke. It took three hours of hard work in the broiling sun to unload the truck and fix the spring. About an hour later, the same trouble happened to one of the trailers and we had to stop and remove the fenders to keep them from rubbing through the tires.

We finally got under way and arrived in Dinder where we filled our water cans. Puppy got rambunctious again and bit another native. We had to explain things all over again to the police. The native was satisfied when we gave him a couple of pounds of coarse salt and put some band-aids on the bites. The diet of the natives in this part of the country is so salt deficient, they consider it as a great delicacy and eat it by the handfuls, like a little boy in a sugar bowl.

There are huge flocks of big ravens along the road. Cass was showing off and dropped two of them with my over-under shotgun. Jim, not to be outdone, fired at one, which sailed away amid a shower of black feathers. Jim looked after the bird and after a moment said, with no change of expression:

"Gentlemen, you have just witnessed a miracle; yonder flies a dead bird."

The country is becoming increasingly rough. We are in an area of small hills, which are covered with coarse brown grass. Some of this grass is as tall as the cab of the truck. In other places the grass has been burned off for thousands of acres. I'd sure hate to get caught in a fire in this place. The road petered out to a mere trail and now that is gone and we are heading cross country, trusting to our compass for direction. It is mighty hot here, too, as little breeze stirs in the tall grass. You can't see where you are driving half the time and it's not unusual to hit a stump or a big rock before you can stop. The seeds from the tall grass are hitting the windshields and roofs of the vehicles like hail. The only fact which keeps us from feeling discouraged is that the country is beginning to look like hunting country for the first time.

We began to see some game shortly after noon. Several dik-dik, as well as some Grant's, and tommies. Once in a dense underbrush, we saw a lovely sable as he dashed across ahead of the convoy. He is one of the most magnificent of the antelope family, rivalled only by the major kudu. Unlike most antelopes, his neck arches while running, so that he looks like a champion horse. He is not as fast a runner as some of the other antelopes and is usually found in thinly forested country just like the area we are passing through now. He likes good cover with plenty of sunlight. When frightened he snorts like a horse and he is one of the few antelopes who will fight if cornered.

Both the male and female have beautiful sickle-shaped horns which sweep back from he head for a distance of up to 64 inches. These horns are as sharp as sword points and the sable will use them efficiently in self-defense. A full-grown male will stand 54 inches at the shoulder and weigh 450 pounds. The females and young are reddish brown, with white markings on the muzzle and about the eyes. A mature male will be almost black. The sable often travels in herds of up to twenty animals with only one herd bull. The older bulls and bachelors with no harem run together.

About four o'clock, we came to the brow of a little hill. Here we were on the edge of some burned-out country. The grass had regrown so that it was about waist deep. We ran head-on into a herd of eighteen tiang, or "horse antelope" as they are sometimes called. They get this title from the fact their face looks something like that of a horse with horns.

I was driving the truck at this time, so I sat back and watched the boys try out their shooting eyes for the first time. I wasn't too impressed by what I saw. The colonel was using his Weatherby .300 magnum, an excellent weapon. He blazed away for several shots without hitting anything except the dirt. Later, when he had the chance to check his sights, he found the scope had been knocked off zero by the constant jarring of the vehicle. This is a common complaint among African hunters and one which can cause a good deal of trouble. Unless a weapon is carried in a first-class rifle rack which will protect it from all shocks, the sight will become jarred out of line and will invariably be "off-target."

Because of this, I preferred to use an open iron sight on my rifle. I found that a majority of my shots were within 150 yards range and I could hit with accuracy at that distance. I wouldn't recommend a peep sight, for it is often difficult to use due to the shimmering heat waves encountered in most African hunting. On my Savage .308 light rifle, I found a 2x by 9x variable scope worked the best. I used a mount where the telescope sight could be easily dismounted and I would carry the sight in my pocket until I got ready to hunt. This way it was always sighted in properly.

Willy dropped a fine buck and Jim, not to be outdone, wounded another and it took us the best part of an hour to run him down. By the time the animals were dressed, the sun had begun to drop behind the trees and we knew we had better make camp.

We stopped in a grove of trees which was loaded with colobus monkeys and an unusual little fellow with long fiery red hair. The colobus or bishop monkey as they are sometimes called are pretty animals. Their skins are in demand for ceremonial robes and for the making of rugs. They have a cape of long black and white hair which hangs over their shoulders like an outer garment.

While some of us helped pitch camp, the younger fellows went out in search of camp meat. Jim came in thirty minutes later with sixteen guineas, while Harv had shot a nice tender shoat.

After sponging off the dirt and having something to eat, the morale of the crowd went up 100 per cent. All but me. I was too sick to eat, or care about much of anything. I was running a high fever and was beginning to get chills which were reminiscent of the malaria I'd had back in World War II while in the Pacific. I was hopeful it was not a return, for I had not had an attack for ten years and I had been taking my atabrine tablets faithfully. While the other boys sat around the fire, I climbed into my bedroll, piled on the blankets and was miserable.

Sleep came slow to me. For the first time I realized how much we depended on doctors and other modern conveniences. To add to the difficulties of sleeping, the sounds of the African night seemed to be increased. The hyenas seemed to be louder, the lions' roar closer, and the monkeys more restless. As near as I could figure, we were on the south bank of the Dinder River, in the vicinity of the Dinder National Game Preserve.

February 9, 1962: We left camp this morning. The boys wanted to look over the country before they left, and as I felt pretty bad anyway, I stayed in bed and let them go without any fuss. Fadul made some hot soup from guinea breasts and that helped a bit. When we got started, we had been on the road less than an hour when we ran into our first roan antelope. Next to the kudu and the sable, this is one of the loveliest animals in Africa. The roan is slightly larger than the sable, but its horns are shorter and not so spectacular. Its horns seldom exceed thirty inches in length. A big roan will stand five feet at the front shoulder and tip the scales at 600 pounds. The male has a grizzled, roan-colored coat, which is much different from the bull sable. The animal is also a good fighter if cornered. These animals travel together in herds and when galloping, look and sound much like horses. They prefer the rolling country which is not very thickly wooded. We saw herds of these lovely animals which numbered as many as sixty.

Late that afternoon, we saw signs of buffalo and one place where it looked as though lion might have been around. The boys are getting itchy trigger fingers. I'm just existing. What a miserable way to spend a trip you have spent a lifetime anticipating.

Just before dark, we ran into a party of Italians from Khartoum. They had just shot a fine roan bull and we stopped to look it over. They told us the location of a fine hunting camp not too far away and we headed there without delay. This will probably be a permanent camp and we may be here for several weeks. It is one of the finest camp sites I have ever seen and the hunting country around here is nothing short of gorgeous.

Our camp grounds are on the bank of a little stream which is only a short distance from the Blue Nile. The site of the main camp is under a huge thorn tree which must be at least thirty feet in diameter and whose shade covers at least half an acre of ground. There are huge roots coming out from the main trunk and these make fine benches. I set up my cot under a low hanging branch which will give me plenty of shade all day long and is an ideal place to hang my mosquito netting. By driving a few nails into the limb, I have plenty of room to hang up my gear. We are only 100 feet or so from a lovely pool which must cover five acres.

It appears to be fed by underground springs and is cool and sweet. It will make an ideal place to bathe and will be handy for our water supply. Even feeling as bad as I do now, I'd like to wash off some of the accumulated dirt. Guess I better wait until I get over this cold, as I'd hate to have it turn into pneumonia.

February 10, 1962: This morning, quite early, we signed on two local boys to help as guides. Old Twenty Pounds is furious, as he wants to be the head man. The new men are brothers from a nomad tribe, names Abdullah and Mohammed. They have agreed to work for us for thirty days for one empty gasoline drum and the excess meat from the animals we kill. They dry the meat and make something like biltong, or the pemmican of our American Indians.

Mohammed is wearing a beret Willy gave him. With a bandoleer of ammunition draped over his shoulder and carrying my double barrel shotgun, he makes a mighty warlike figure. Only his bare feet and legs seem out of place.

The two boys follow us around like pet dogs and we have to talk to them through the use of hand and arm signals when Abraham or Fadul aren't around. It is amazing how soon you learn to communicate in this manner.

Late this afternoon, I was feeling so much better I took Abdullah to the swimming hole with me. I gave him a bar of Camay soap and showed him how to use it. When I left thirty minutes later, he was still soaping himself and washing off the suds; the soap fascinates him and he loves the smell. Two hours later, he came back to camp, having used up the entire bar of soap. We had to put him on a strict ration of a bar a week, for the first couple of days he spent all his time at the "old swimmin' hole" and used up a bar of soap a day. That boy had never been as clean in his life, nor had he ever smelled as good.

February 11, 1962: Got up early this morning and after

a breakfast of pig steaks, pancakes, and six fried eggs washed down with a gallon of hot coffee, I took off through a burned-out area with Harv. We saw a good many oribi, guinea fowl, and two herds of wart hogs. About ten o'clock we saw a good bush buck and Harv got a standing shot at him from about 200 yards but missed. Looks like his sight is off too.

The bushbuck or harnessed antelope as he is sometimes called is a very timid animal and it is unusual to see them in the open country. Usually they travel in pairs and are seldom seen during the daylight hours. Most often if you see them at all, it will be just as darkness is setting in and then usually near the edge of a heavily wooded area. It is one of the wariest of all African antelopes and will take to the water when pursued, as it is a fine swimmer. In spite of its wary nature, it is rather noisy and utters a deep bark when disturbed. The males will vary in color from nearly black to a bright chestnut. The one we saw was almost golden color, with two white stripes on its side running horizontally on its ribs. It has several white spots on the hips and white markings on the chest and is a beautiful little animal. A mature buck will stand about thirty inches high, and have spiral horns which will seldom exceed eighteen inches in length. It feeds in open range country bordering forest-lands.

We got back late that afternoon to find that Willy and Jim had come in with two nice reedbuck and two pigs. These reedbuck are also solitary creatures and are seldom seen during daylight. They feed mostly at night and in the early morning and are never seen in herds. The reedbuck differs from the other antelopes in that it seldom is found far from water. When alarmed, it gives a sharp whistle. All the reedbucks I saw were about the same size as a white-tailed deer and were yellowish in color. Their horns are black ringed and spread up and to the front for a maximum of sixteen inches.

Later that afternoon, Harv and the colonel went out for a while and came in about dark with a fine bull Tiang the colonel had shot. The carcasses of the tiang and reedbuck will be used for leopard bait.

We know there are leopard about, as we have seen plenty of signs along the river and within a mile of camp. Every night we hear at least two of them in the vicinity.

Many hunters class the leopard at the top of the list of most dangerous game and there are some fine arguments about it. I guess a man who has been clawed by a leopard would be inclined to place him there. Personally, I feel as though cape buffalo is the toughest, although I'd not argue with the leopard man.

The leopard is the most difficult of all African game to hunt. He is not as large as the lion, seldom weighing over 150 pounds, but he is every ounce a devil and is usually much more aggressive than a lion. Add up his exceptional sense of sight and hearing, to a finely tuned nose; multiply this by the wisdom of the devil and you have a tough, dangerous combination. The leopard is one animal which will not hesitate a bit when it comes to attacking a hunter.

Because of these attributes, it is not an easy thing to select the best site for a hunting blind. First the bait tree must be selected with special care. You can't go up to the first tree handy and use it. You must find a tree which is near water and which has good cover nearby. If the tree is too far from cover, the intelligent animal will leave it strictly alone, no matter how juicy the bait. This tree must have a limb parallel to the ground and is large enough so the leopard can lay full length and eat in comfort.

Secondly, there must be good cover for the hunter near the bait tree. Usually the hunter will want to use another tree within thirty yards of the bait for his stand. It is necessary for the stand to be this close, as at night and with excellent camouflage, you will not be able to pick up the cat from farther away. I've sat watching the bait for hours with nothing stirring, then suddenly you look closer and the cat is there. You saw no movement, or heard no sound, but the feline appeared as though by magic. Sometimes a good camouflaged position can be found at ground level, but many hunters do not like this, as leopards have been known to attack the ambushed hunters in their blind. The camouflage on the blind must be near perfect—natural camouflage is the best—or the beast will recognize the danger immediately. The concealment must be downwind, not only from the bait tree, but also from the beast's likely avenue of approach.

You can see that it is no easy matter to find the proper location. We were lucky and found an ideal spot, less than a mile from camp. After we dragged the bait to the tree and securely lashed it in place, we left for the night. It would probably be several days before the cat investigated it, as they like their meat to be a "bit high."

We were still relaxing from the trip. I was beginning to feel a bit more human, although I tired readily. At least I am beginning to enjoy the good food which Fadul was putting out for us. That boy is an absolute wizard when it comes to cooking over an open fire. We still have some fresh vegetables and yesterday Abdullah brought us twenty fresh eggs.

February 12, 1962: After a good dinner and a smoke, I fell asleep at once. It seemed as though I had hardly closed my eyes when Fadul was shaking me by the shoulder.

"There are some men here who want to see you sir," he said, "one of them is sick and needs help."

I rolled out of the bedroll into a frosty morning and made my way to where the fire was blazing cheerfully. I didn't realize it then, but I was about to embark on a new phase of my life in Africa.

Several villianous-looking individuals with spears were gathered around the fire. With them was a pretty, light-skinned girl of possibly fourteen or fifteen. She had spilled hot grease over herself and was badly burned from her left elbow to her knees. Some of the flesh was so badly burned that it had been cooked and cracked.

I spent most of the remaining hours of the night dressing the burn with sulfa and salve from my first aid kit. Possibly I worked a bit slower than usual, and I must have been feeling a good deal better, for I was uncomfortably aware that the girl was beautiful and was wearing an absolute minimum of clothing.

One of the older men, her father, told me through Fadul, that he had a terrible pain in his head. I gave him ten aspirin with directions how to use them. He promptly put them in his mouth and chewed them up. I guess he had the same attitude some other people have. If the medicine tastes bad enough, it must be good. He was back in an hour, hand to head, begging for more pills.

The coffee was sending off tantalizing odors by now, when I noticed more natives had gathered around the fire, until about twenty-five of the evil-smelling fellows clustered about. They were eyeing me in a most suspicious manner. When they put their heads together and began to whisper, my guilty conscience got the better of me and said that I may have overdone the admiring glances I had spent on the Sudanese belle.

Finally my nervousness got the better of me and I asked Fadul what they were saying:

"Nothing much," he said. "They say that you truly great hakim. In their language that means doctor. They think you very great and kind man."

I breathed a sigh of relief. After this I became known as "The Hakim." More and more my nights and siestas were interrupted by medical treatment periods. It was lucky I had brought plenty of first aid materials along. It became something of a nuisance, but I was getting quite a spiritual uplift from helping my fellowman. Sometimes there were as many as thirty people waiting when I got back to camp.

Late one night, a young warrior was brought into camp with a terrible wound. He had been thrown from a camel and had landed on his spear point. The iron blade had torn through muscle and blood vessel to the bone and had laid his arm open from the wrist to elbow. I took one look at it and told Abe, "I'm not that good a doctor, Abe, I can't sew up blood vessels."

"You must," he said, "or the man will die anyway."

I guess I did some praying that night. I wasn't afraid of what might happen if the man died. I only knew I had many limitations as far as being a doctor was concerned and that a human life was in my hands.

There was no pain killer to administer, but with the help of the camp boys, who made willing if clumsy assistants, we set to work. Working by the light of two gasoline lanterns, I sewed up torn muscles and blood vessels, using a darning needle and fifteen pound test monofilament fishing line. Somewhere in Sudan today, if he is still alive, is a Sudanese native held together with American fishing line. The last I heard, he was getting along fine.

Every hour I spent working with these people, I realized how fortunate we Americans are in the care we receive. I began to see why missionaries say it is important first to administer to man's need, then to his soul.

I was touched by the way these simple people showed their gratitude. I asked for no pay and in most cases they could have afforded nothing. We were kept in good supply with eggs, fresh vegetables, and even chickens. One man even offered me his thirteen-year-old daughter after I had treated his wife. I am the honorary godfather of several Sudanese boys and girls, a position which came about through assisting at their births. I tried in the short time I was there to instill a few fundamental ideas of sanitation in their minds: such as the use of boiled clothes and boiling water during child birth. A high percentage of mothers and babies are lost at birth due to sepsis. In a short time, I heard many a murmured:

"Hakim, al hamdullillah!" Literally translated it means: "The blessings of God on the doctor."

Now that we were settled in camp, we fell into a more or less regular schedule. Usually we would go out in two's or three's, using the two Rovers. Most of the hunting would be in the early morning or late evening, although sometimes we would get so far from camp in the morning we would stay all day and many times it was long after dark before we got back.

There is something reassuring about a campfire. You leave early in the morning to hunt all day and come back after dark, bone tired and covered with the dirt of the day's driving. Suddenly through the darkness, you see a pinpoint of light. You know it is your campfire and that soon you will be able to relax and enjoy a good hot meal. As you get closer, the heavenly aroma of coffee drifts downwind to you on the gentle evening breeze, mixed in with the delicious odor of fresh biscuits and frying steaks. You know then you are home.

February 13, 1962: By the evening of this day, I still hadn't fired a shot except to zero in my rifle. Harv and the colonel came in from a hard day in the tall grass country. They had seen plenty of game including two lion, but had not been able to get into shooting range of any of it. We do not hunt from our vehicles. When game is sighted, we dismount and move up on foot. If it is dangerous game such as buffalo or lion, we try to get within a maximum of seventy-five yards. For other game the maximum is 150 yards. Sometimes this won't work out, but for dangerous game it is almost an unwritten law.

In this way, very little game is wounded and allowed to escape into the bush. Big game can be knocked down with the first shot and then kept there, if the hunter is a good shot, gets close enough, and uses his head. In thirty days of hunting there was only one wounded animal which got away into the brush. One night Harv hit a big pig just at dark and it got away into the thick brush where we could not follow it. The next day, we found it partially eaten by some animal.

I was feeling a whole lot better by now and got up enough gumption to take the Rover down to the water hole for filling the cans. Promptly got mired and had to have old Death and Destruction winch me out.

February 14, 1962: Willy, Jim, and I went out early this morning and got into some fine country. We saw lots of oribi, reedbuck and a few fine water buck. Also ran into a nice herd of tiang, some 47 animals. I dropped two of them on the run, with the .338 performing beautifully at 347 and 318 paces. It only takes one shot from the .338 in the right place to knock most game head over heels.

We ran into the first buffaloes we had seen and Willy got chased by the big bull I told about in Chapter 8. Had one devil of a time getting the big fellow into the back of the Rover and finally ended by cutting off the hind quarters, some of the sirloin, and the head. That enormous head must have weighed at least 300 pounds as it was all two of us could do to load it.

The bait we put into the tree has been tampered with and we can see claw marks from a big leopard who had been working around the bait tree. Guess it is "high" enough now so it will pay to put a night watch on the stand. We decided to change off with two or three men watching each night. This gives the hunters protection and also saves on a lot of lost sleep.

After sitting in the blind for my share of a week and seeing none of the elusive animals, although we knew they were around, I decided to take a night off and go after some of the big wart hogs which were feeding in the native maize fields just out from camp. This was the night I shot the two leopards I told about in Chapter 7. These were the only two leopards shot during this trip. One of the boys got a shot at one in the bait tree one night and missed. Shooting with the use of a light is tricky business, especially when dealing with a leopard, for the cats are so fast you only have a split second to aim and fire before they are out of range.

Februray 15, 1962: We went far afield today and got a fine bag of tiang and one nice reedbuck. On the way home, we bogged down in the riverbed, sinking the Rover in the sand until it rested on its frame. It was hot as the dickens and after sweating for two hours in the blazing sun, we took time out to go swimming in a pothole nearby.

Just as we got out of the water, three big Sudanese men came by. They were very friendly and helped us push the car out of the sand trap. It is nice to find people who will help without expecting to be paid. They refused the money we offered and settled for a package of cigarettes.

They were intrigued with book matches and I gave them several folders I had in the Rover. Somewhere along the line those men must have met some American GI's, for while they were leaning against the car smoking, one of them looked at me and said:

"You comprende shithouse?" This is a most un-British expression.

Abdullah was with us and as a result all our talking was in hand and arm signals. Willy trying to be friendly patted the side of the Rover and said:

"Jeepo!"

One of the coal black natives grinned from ear to ear and patted the car saying:

"Land Rover." This broke us up, because of the silly look on Big William's face. This seemed to be the extent of their English, but we parted the best of friends. The more I see of these people, the better I like them.

Our game bag is beginning to fill up. One of the boys came in with a fine zebra pelt which will make a lovely rug. There do not seem to be many zebras in this area.

Late in the afternoon the colonel and Harv came in with the first roan antelope shot on the trip. The colonel got the big bull with one shot and it will surely be big enough to go into the record book. I got a lucky shot at a nice impala and dropped him.

Willy, Jim, and I got in early and spent the rest of a hot afternoon changing oil and greasing the vehicles in the shade of a big thorn tree.

The Rovers have proved to be superior hunting vehicles. Before I got mine, I spent many miles traveling by military jeep. Personally my vote goes to the Rover as a hunting vehicle. They are much more comfortable to ride over rough ground due to a superior suspension system. This also aids in the driving qualities. Because their wheels are a bit farther apart than those of a jeep, they are more stable on extremely rough terrain. One problem of the jeep is its tendency to roll in a sharp turn, or on a steep side hill. The Rovers also seem to stand up better under the severe pounding we give them day after day.

February 16, 1962: This afternoon, while chasing a herd of roan antelope cross country with Jim at the wheel, we hit a big log which was concealed in the tall grass. Although we were traveling close to forty miles an hour at the time, no damage was done other than a severe jolting and a bent bumper. The vehicle jumped the log and I ended up on the hood, with our gear piled over and on me.

Found several patients waiting for me when I got back. One young fellow had a nasty-looking leg which was infected with screw worms. These worms, dead white in color, are the size of a pencil lead and up to five inches long. They were embedded the full length into the calf of his leg. I don't know what causes them, but they sure do make a nasty-looking sore.

February 17, 1962: Today we drove fifty miles to visit the game commissioner at the National Preserve. He is a coal black native, dressed English fashion and speaking English with an Oxford accent. He was a graduate of Oxford University in 1956. He treated us with the gravest of courtesy and seemed happy to meet us. Some of his tips on lion hunting in the area were helpful and resulted in two fine, full-maned lion before the trip was over. On our way back to camp, Willy shot the largest roan bull we got during the trip.

We also got two more fine impalas. This animal is without a doubt the loveliest of a beautiful family of animals and certainly the most graceful. I'm not sure, but I believe it will classify as the fastest runner in this family also. In full steam, they will bound over big rocks and bushes with little apparent effort. In jumping, the impala seem to float through the air. Sometimes when a herd is in motion, they will bound over each other. They can clear an eight-foot fence with ease. The impala's coat is a reddish gold, with white underparts. Their ringed, lyre-shaped horns may reach up to twenty inches.

February 18, 1962: To supplement our food supply, Harv and I took our fishing gear and drove the fifteen miles to the main channel of the Blue Nile. I had along a deep-sea trolling rig with forty-pound test and a Mitchell 302, Salt Water Spinning rig with twenty pound monofilament. We came back that night with a fine 35-pound catfish and the picture of a 125-pound Nile perch we had landed. The record for Nile perch is something like 545 pounds and 150-pound catfish are not unusual.

It is exciting fishing here, for it is not at all unusual to hook a perch or catfish and have it become bait for a big croc. When this happens you lose both hook and bait, as no forty-pound line will hold one of these monsters in a river.

I also encountered an unusual type eel. This fellow got tangled in my line and when I tried to get him unwrapped, I received an electric shock which knocked me flat and scared the dickens out of me. Several natives standing by thought this was very funny. One of them spoke a bit of English and told us that these big eels grow to a length of twenty feet and will stun a horse with their electric current.

While here, we met an Italian plantation owner. During

our conversation, we heard a few of the unusual native sayings which are common in this area:

When you have a flat tire the native says: "Your car has sore feet." When it thunders: "God is angry." If it hails, as it does sometimes in this area: "God is throwing stones at us." Ice is called: "Water that has gone to sleep."

I noticed that natives coming in contact with modern inventions were sometimes a bit confused. We saw the driver of a big lorry, loaded with cotton, standing beside the truck. It had stalled for some reason and the driver was beating the hood with a big stick, as he would a reluctant camel.

February 18–26, 1962: Normal hunting activities during this period, with two lions bagged by the colonel and Harv.

Several fine waterbuck and reedbuck trophies have been brought in and two more big bull roans.

Seems as though I'm spending more and more time with my medical work, but I don't mind it. Just to see the gratitude of the natives, who have to depend on a witch doctor for help, is more than enough pay. I wonder if some of the local witch doctors aren't a bit jealous of Hakim Mohr. Maybe I'd better watch out, or I'll be the subject of a hex.

February 27, 1962: Received a message from the Sudanese police who drove 250 km cross country to locate our camp. They relayed a message which came through the American Embassy at Khartoum. We are to get in touch with Kagnew Station at once.

Everyone was worried about it, especially those who had families in Asmara. Harv, Willy, and the colonel drove the 250 km to Singa to find out what the message was all about.

While they were gone, Jim and I went out and came back with the only sable shot during the trip. Jim made a

one-shot kill of the big bull which was under a full head
of steam at 385 paces. It was one of the finest shots I've
seen.

The other party got back about eleven P.M. They were
pretty well beaten up by the trip. Their news was unwelcome, for it means the end of the trip for the colonel and
me. We have to return for official army business.

February 28, 1962: Cass and I left at nine this morning,
but hadn't got clear of camp when our generator burned
out. Came back and put in a new one and started out
again. The main road has been graded in our absence and
outside of the dust which is as bad as ever, the return trip
is much better. We made it to Gedaref the first night and
were visited by the police commissioner. One of the first
things he asked about was how the yellow dog was getting
along.

The weather has cooled off some.

March 1, 1962: When we arrived in Kassala, it was to
find the governor had helped us again by smoothing our
way through customs. We arrived in Tessenai about two
o'clock. For no apparent reason, Eritrean customs office was
closed. It finally reopened at five and we had a bit of
trouble explaining why there were only two of us coming
out of Sudan. Finally convinced them we weren't trying
to do anything illegal and left. In spite of the danger from
shiftas and this is a bad area for the bandits, we drove
straight through to Cheren, arriving about nine. We had
made over 600 km on the rough, dusty roads and the hot
bath sure felt fine. The meal which followed was even
better, as we had subsisted on Tootsie Rolls and crackers
all that day.

The rest of our group arrived back at Kagnew Station
on March 10. All the pelts came through in excellent shape,

which was a real credit to Abraham's skill as a skinner. The trip more than filled our expectations. Here is a run-down of expenses for the forty-day trip:

Insurance on Vehicles	$ 33.60
Five hunting licenses	$ 85.00
Food	$199.70
Gasoline (542 gal)	$133.10
3 bags of charcoal	$ 2.40
Repairs on three tires	$ 3.00
Customs at Kassala	$ 4.80
200 kg salt	$ 12.00
Camp help (cook and skinner)	$ 80.00
Rental of truck and trailers	$120.00
Vehicle parts	$ 10.00
Misc.	$ 6.00
TOTAL	**$689.80**

Average per man ran $137.96 for the forty days. This was well below the $1,000 limit we had set. This sum did not include mounting of trophies. In my case, the twelve trophies I brought back cost me about $150.00.

14
General Observations on African Hunting

I would like to conclude the hunting portion of this book with some general observations.

Many Americans make themselves miserable while traveling in a foreign country through their own ignorance. No matter where you travel—and I have been in thirty-five different countries—you will be warned about dangers you may encounter from food and drink. These dangers are justified, but should be taken with a grain of common sense.

I recall one American lady in Asmara, who had used eggs from the commissary for two years. One day, she found that they were laid by Eritrean chickens. Immediately she stopped using them and went back to powdered eggs. This type of thinking is sort of juvenile.

In all my travels abroad, the only time I was ever troubled with stomach ailment due to food or water was in Korea in 1948, when I got a fine case of dysentery while eating at a GI mess hall in Seoul.

The natives of most countries are very generous and will

try and be friendly with you if you let them. In some of the larger cities, you will find a lot of communist influence and these are the cities where you see the "Go Home Yankee," signs.

In fourteen years spent outside the United States, I can't recall a single time when I was in serious trouble with the natives of any country I lived in or visited. I always went on the assumption that most people will go out of their way in extending you courtesies, if you in turn will be considerate and courteous. I have been invited into many native homes in many countries and have participated in many unusual and very interesting customs. Sometimes it's better not to know what you are eating or drinking, as in the case of the fermented camel's milk, but I've always managed to survive and have made a lot of good friends in the process.

Visitors who observe local customs will usually find the natives warm and friendly. Never let it show that you consider home customs to be better than theirs, even though it may be so.

Many American tourists have a tic, which might be called "United States-itis." I have seen this disease in operation all over the world and it's fatal towards real friendship.

"Our sky scrapers are bigger," they say. "Our highways are finer, our sanitary conditions better and you just can't compare your homes to ours, you know."

Or maybe they will say:

"That isn't the way we do it in the States"; or, "We never do it that way at home." Over and over ad nauseam. Undoubtedly they are right in this one respect. Home was never like this, but that's why they are making the trip, isn't it? To see something new and different. There is absolutely no point in traveling anywhere in a foreign country, if you are going to be a carbon copy of the United States while you are there. The delight is in the difference. I don't mean you should run down your country. People who do that are as bad as the ones who go to the opposite extreme and will come in for their share of foreign contempt.

Most visitors coming to a foreign country arrive in a healthy frame of mind, where they are anxious to learn as much as possible about the country and to get along well with its natives. Still, there are some of our good citizens who hardly step off the plane at a new destination before they are attacked by a nervous condition which seems to force them into an irresistible comparison of everything they see, with that which they understand from their own country. Usually this is accompanied by a discussion in loud, obnoxious tones which can be heard all over a hotel lobby or restaurant; obviously distaining all the things they see. These people are unwelcome in any place whether it is Oslo, Paris, Madrid, Rome, Addis Ababa, Nairobi, Tokyo, Hongkong, or any other place. Unfortunately, even lavish tipping will not make up for this obvious lack of breeding.

You will find it well worth your time to learn a few phrases in the language of the country you are visiting: "hello," "good-morning," "how are you," when said with a smile, will go a long way toward making genuine friends.

Another "pet peeve" of mine is the American who flashes a big bankroll, while in loud, sometimes vulgar terms, he lets everyone within hearing know just what a "big shot" he is back home. He's doing more than putting himself in the category of Americans that are not welcome and which cause the "Hate America" signs to be written all over the world. He's making a genuine ass out of himself and fooling no one.

I have a motto, which has served me well. When I arrive in a new country, I try and act in such a way the natives will be able to say:

"All Americans aren't as bad as we've been led to believe. He is the nicest American we've ever met."

There is a health problem in Africa; no question about that. There are also health problems in many places in the United States. With a little preparation and use of a little common sense, there is very little to fear. If you have the proper shots and use normal sanitary precautions, you will have very little to worry about. Don't let over anxiety spoil the fun of your trip.

We have discussed some of the obvious dangers in Africa, from animals, insects, and reptiles. I would venture to say, you would be safer walking across Africa without firearms, than you would be to wander on the side streets of Washington, D.C., after dark.

Let's spend a few paragraphs discussing firearms and their uses. If I ever go on another hunting trip to Africa, and I fervently hope this will be possible, I will obtain any guns needed from the safari company which arranges my trip. This eliminates a great deal of red tape in arranging for import and export licenses and insures the use of the proper type of firearm. It is disappointing for a man to bring his favorite Weatherby .300 all the way to Africa and then find he cannot use it against such animals as buffalo.

If you decide to take your own guns, here are a few tips which may be helpful:

Be sure to take along a shotgun, preferably a double over-under. This is a necessity for procuring much delicious food for the camp and is also a lot of fun. Sometimes when a man has spent several days of intense big game hunting in the bush it is a great relaxer to get the smooth bore and do some bird hunting. The double is unexcelled if you have to go into heavy bush after a leopard. Take along a .22 rifle and plenty of ammunition for plinking and bird hunting.

For lighter game such as the gazelle and antelope, rifles in the .30 caliber class are good. You don't need a magnum for these types of game and the lighter rifle is a lot more fun to fire. I was well pleased with the performance of my Savage, model 99F, in .308 caliber. Mounted with a 2x by 9x variable scope, this weapon did everything I asked of it and in a superior manner. I liked the lever action, as it is faster for me than the bolt action and I was often able to get off an extra shot. This is important to keep a wounded animal from escaping into the bush.

Much has been said about the heavier bore rifles vs the fast muzzle velocity magnums. There is no question in my mind, that the superior rifles for hunting big game in Africa are the heavy bore guns. Every kind of African game has been killed by the .30 rifle, but it does not meet the need of the average hunter and is illegal to use against some of the tougher game in several areas. This goes for the .300 magnums also.

Without much doubt, the finest big game guns made anywhere in the world are the English double rifles. Their price will set you back almost as much as the average thirty-day safari. These guns range from .400 to over .500 caliber. The average-sized man will not want to fire more than three or four shots a day from one of these heavy-weights, as their kick on the butt end is almost as strong as their power from the front.

There are two American made bolt-action rifles now available which have performed well on African big game. These are the .375 magnum and the African .458 magnum.

The big African will fire a bullet up to 500 grains in weight and that is a heck of a lot of lead. The beauty of both these guns is that they can be purchased for less than $500. Weatherby also has a fine gun in similar bore size.

One thing to remember about a scope is this. If you have traveled very far, over rough terrain with a scoped rifle, better check before firing it at game. The chances are it will need to be re-zeroed. We learned this the hard way on our Sudan trip, when we lost some fine trophies before it dawned on us what was wrong with our guns.

If you use a scope, it is advisable to have one which will either tip off, or is quickly detachable. With dangerous game, in heavy brush, the scope isn't much good and can be dangerous.

Another good tip to remember has been mentioned before. When hunting for dangerous animals, get as close as possible to the quarry, knock it down with the first shot, and then keep it down. Few hunters have been hurt by an animal which has been kept off its feet.

If you are hunting with a professional guide, as you most undoubtedly will, he will give you all the professional advice necessary for your safety. Listen to him. Sometimes you may resent his care a bit, but remember he is responsible for your safety and he can easily lose his guide's license if something should happen to you. If you want to have fun and get the most out of your trip, plus getting the best trophies, act as much like a well-mannered human being as is possible. Remember the White Hunter with you is human too and he will respond with greater efforts if you treat him right. Don't try and impress him with your importance. It probably won't work, for most of these men have worked with all classes of people including royalty and are not easily impressed.

If you want to impress your hunter, there is nothing which will impress him more than plain old fashioned "guts." The man who panics in a moment of danger—the man who wounds a dangerous animal and then refuses to help dispose of it—is looked on with contempt, no matter what his station in life, or how big his bankroll.

An African safari is no place to practice up for "Lost Weekends." If you have to hit the bottle, stay home, don't do it on your hunting trip. On most custom safaris, liquor is optional, but more disagreeable incidents come from drunken clients than from any other source.

It might be of interest to discuss here a little bit about the present hunting situation in Africa, as far as game conservation is concerned.

Recent political changes have made the future of the wild animals of Africa far worse than envisaged a short time ago. Some experts say the numbers of African big game, except for those in primeval forests, have sunk to less than 20 per cent of what they were before the Europeans appeared on the scene during the second half of the nineteenth century. There seems to be little danger of the larger animals such as the leopard, lion, elephant, hippopotamus, buffalo, giraffe, etc., vanishing and becoming extinct as was the case with the American bison, unless something totally unexpected happens.

Public demands are often made for the reduction in number of certain carnivorous animals—partly for safeguarding of rare species of game. The weight of public opinion in favor of their preservation is strong. Most visitors to East Africa show an overwhelming interest in seeing and photographing the larger beasts. Other animals like the antelope and gazelle are often ignored. When visitors to a national park complain: "We've seen nothing again today," it usually means they have seen no lion or elephant. There may have been thousands of lesser animals about.

Although wildlife conservation has been carried out in a haphazard manner in most African countries there is still hope in the new countries such as Kenya, Uganda, and Tanzania.

Because "Primitive Africa" is a great attraction to thousands of tourists and is therefore an important factor in the strained economy of African states, greater efforts are being made to protect their game. The toughest job seems to be to educate the indigenous personnel in cooperating with their own governments.

Due to rigid supervision over foreign sportmen, exercised by both game officials and professional hunters, the danger of game extinction from this viewpoint can be minimized. It is an undisputed fact that illegal hunting by natives is responsible for the greatest percentage of deaths among wild animals.

It is difficult to convince natives of these countries, most of whom are illiterate, that it is just to punish them for killing wild animals, when they see foreigners doing it. The fact that the foreign hunter is spending thousands of dollars for this privilege and that this money goes into game conservation is lost on them.

Unfortunately tens of thousands of animals are killed yearly by native poachers for their skins. Many times the meat is wasted. It is the old idea all over again of "killing the goose that laid the golden egg."

With few exceptions, animals captured for zoos, circuses, etc., play a very minor part in the decreasing of any given species.

Fortunately, many sportsmen are beginning to entertain the same idea I now have. This is that it is more fun and takes more skill to photograph wild animals than it does to shoot them. With the advent of modern photographic equipment, even an amateur can do a good professional job.

The thrill of stalking a dangerous wild animal is still there. The danger is, I believe, greater. It takes more "plain guts" to get close to a cape buffalo, for instance, with a movie camera in your hands, than if you were armed with a .458 rifle. When you become a photographer, you must depend on someone else for your safety. This takes a great deal of faith on your part.

The thrill of showing colored pictures you have taken yourself is as great as that of pointing to a mounted trophy and saying: "I got that one in Sudan during my '64 trip."

The number of animals and their species you can find in some of the great national parks is astonishing. During the course of a day's drive, it is not unusual for a person to see guinea fowl, bustard, ostrich, several types of cats, lion, elephant, zebra, warthogs, gemsbok, nyala, lechwe, kudu, impala, grysbok, wildebeeste, waterbuck, duiker, klipspringer, giraffe, cape buffalo, hyena and jackal. All this in one day and a chance to photograph twenty-four or twenty-five varieties of birds and animals. No hunter could possibly come close to matching this in number of daily trophies.

Because photographing safaris can be accomplished in a shorter time and with much less equipment; because there is no need for guns, ammunition, and preparation of hides and heads, costs are notably lower. Then, too, no little cost of a hunting safari is eaten up in mounting of the trophies when you return home.

According to animal experts, nine species or subspecies of African animals have been lost during the past 2,000 years. This compares with eleven lost on the North American continent. There are now several species of animals in Africa that are in danger of dying out: the white-tailed gnu, mountain zebra, white rhino, the addax, the mountain nyala, and several classes of oryx antelope. Some of these species still exist in protected areas.

The immediate future offers some hope to those of us who are concerned about the preservation of animal life in this greatest of wild game areas.

15 A Note on African Fishing

Before we close, I'd like to put in a brief plug for African fishing.

It may seem strange, but some of the finest trout fishing in the world can be found right here on the equator. The mountain streams of Kenya and other East African countries abound with fighting rainbow trout. A number of years ago, the British introduced ova from rainbow trout into the mountain streams of Mt. Kenya. This ova was flown in from England at a terrific cost and planted at the 11,000-foot level. Today in these streams fish weighing eight or ten pounds are not unusual.

We discussed briefly some of the huge fish which can be caught in the Nile River. I'd like to mention a little about the fishing in the Red Sea and Indian Ocean.

If you were to time your big game safari properly you might also get in some of the finest marlin fishing in the world. Just a couple of hour's drive north of the seaport city of Mombasa in Kenya is the resort city of Malinda Beach. This is a luxury resort which compares favorably with Miami Beach. It is noted for the size and fighting abilities of its giant marlin. Each year a tournament is held here. Boats and equipment are available. The Indian Ocean is also noted for the size of its sharks. Some experts say the largest and most vicious sharks in the world abound in these waters.

Most of my fishing experiences in Africa were in the Red Sea off the coast of Massawa. In the spring of 1961, I met a wonderful American couple who were on their way around the world in their 70-foot sloop the "Sitisi." Bill Lavery had been one of the most successful contractors on the West Coast. Both he and his lovely wife, Mary, became disgusted with the "rat race" of keeping up with the Joneses. They sold their fine home, their car, and furniture and bought the Sitisi. After two years of sailing up and down the California coast, they headed off on their dream voyage, a round the world trip with no passengers other than their two Persian cats.

At Barcelona, Spain, they stopped for several months while Mary taught school at an air force base and Bill chartered out the boat for sailing trips. Finally they reached Massawa on their way through the Red Sea to the Indian Ocean. They were the best, as far as people were concerned, and we became good friends. I had several weeks of leave time coming, so I went on a two week's sailing cruise of the Red Sea islands, lying offshore from Massawa.

The lagoons off many of these islands were fantastic fishing spots. The reefs were often covered by twenty or thirty feet of water, which was as clear as crystal and was the habitat of a multitude of fish. It was not unusual to troll along the edge of one of these reefs and catch as many as four different varieties of fish with one bait. First you might hook a good-sized crevalle, followed by a big grouper; this in turn might be hit by a large barracuda, which in turn would become a victim of a shark. The water was so clear, you could watch all the action—and this added greatly to the excitement.

Many times, you could not troll for more than twenty yards without getting a strike and you never knew what was going to hit your lure. One night, fishing off the dock, I lay my pole down to light a cigar; almost immediately I got a strike which nearly yanked the rod and reel off the pier. Recovering, I set the hook and after quite a tussle brought in a 125-pound tuna. At times the fish would be hitting so fast and furious, you would be tired out within a couple of hours from fighting the fish. When the albacore were hitting, it was not unusual to have three fish on from one boat at the same time. With these greyhounds jumping and moving all around the surface it was some fun to keep from getting lines tangled.

Most of the salt-water fish were fine fighters and many were excellent for table fare. My favorite from the viewpoint of sport were the albacore, king mackerel, and the barracuda. It was not unusual to hook barracuda five feet long.

I did a great deal of skin diving and was amazed at the beauty of underwater coral formations and many different varieties of fish which are not found in the States.

It was not unusual to see a dozen giant manta rays playing on the surface of Massawa Bay, some of these reaching a size of twenty feet. The fishing boats were always bringing in giant shrimp and lobster of the longusta variety.

While fishing off the Dahalact Islands, I had the closest call of all my trips into the field. We left the Sitisi in a small boat to investigate a commotion in the water about two miles away. Something was stirring the water into a froth, shooting spray ten feet or more in the air. When we got closer, we saw it was a huge school of big albacore, possibly in the twenty-pound class, which were jumping frantically out of the water as they tried to elude a big school of sharks. We trolled through this school for half an hour without success, as the albacore seemed more anxious to escape the sharks than to feed. After some time we went back to the sail boat.

While boarding the Sitisi, I fell overboard. Everytime I tried to climb aboard, one of my good friends would push me back into the water. I guess maybe I spent ten minutes trying to climb aboard. Finally they let me get to the ladder and I began to climb out of the water. My feet had barely cleared the water when one of the boys at the rail shouted:

"Shark!"

I drew my feet up as far as I could, just as there was a swirl in the water and I looked down into the face and mouth of a big shark which had missed my dangling legs by inches. To say I was scared is a misnomer. I was petrified. When they hauled me aboard, we threw in three baited lines and within seconds had three fighting sharks boiling up the water about the Sitisi. We were able to land two of the big fish after a battle which lasted thirty minutes. They were in the eight-foot class and all of them had dental ware which could easily have severed my legs. Looking at those pointed teeth, I breathed a prayer of thanksgiving, and was thankful my feet hadn't ended in their stomachs.

Bill and Mary went on to visit the Seychelle Islands in the middle of the Indian Ocean. The last I heard from them was in 1964, when they were in New Guinea.

Fishing in inland waters of Africa was always an exciting experience, for one never knew what to expect, either on the land or in the water. Many times it was necessary to follow an animal trail through thick brush in order to reach the river banks and it was not at all unusual to run head on into an irritable rhino or some mean buffalo who had been drinking at the stream.

One of my good friends spent several hours up a thorn tree one day. He had gone to do some fishing and left his rifle behind—a very foolish thing to do at any time. While heading down a narrow trail towards the river, he ran head on into a big buffalo bull who promptly ran him up a thorn tree. A spinning rod with 15-pound test line is not too good for catching a 2,000 pound buffalo. We reached him in the late afternoon and found him in a foul mood. He was covered from head to foot with scratches from the thorns and the camel flies had been feasting on him unmercifully. His mood was not improved by the wise remarks which were made in camp that night about fishing for buffalo with a spinning rod.

On a fishing day on the Blue Nile, I had a big perch on my Mitchell 302. I was loaded with 200 yards of 20 pound monofilament and was giving the big fish a good fight. For thirty minutes I had run up and down a big sand bar, trying to wear the big fish out. The perch must have weighed over a 100 pounds. Several times I forced him to the surface, where I got a good look at him. It was the biggest freshwater fish I had ever hooked. Not only was the battle exciting, but there is also an element of danger in this type of fishing, as you must keep one eye opened for any crocodiles which may decide to take a hand in the game. Just when I thought I had him licked, there was a big swirl in the water and the rod bent almost double as something hit the perch. The line went strangely slack and in a few seconds I reeled in the remains of my prize fish—the head and about ten inches of body. The rest had been chopped off as cleanly as if someone had used an axe. It must have been a good-sized croc, for the head and part of the body weighed close to thirty pounds.

The excitement of these fishing trips added immeasurably to the fun of fishing. Sometimes a herd of baboon would come close to see what you were doing and one day a big bull elephant came down to water within fifty feet of where I was casting. Then, too, there was always the pleasure of having fresh fish for dinner.

16　It's Worth a Try

Possibly this book has whetted your appetite for big game hunting. I hope it has proved of interest to you and that you have received some enjoyment by reading it.

"I'd love to go to Africa," you may say, "but it's a rich man's game and I just can't afford it."

This was essentially true a few years ago. Today, safari companies are looking longingly towards the tourist trade. The result has been an almost phenomenal drop in safari prices over the last ten years, without any appreciable drop in the excellent services which are offered.

It is quite obvious, I'm sure, that the trips I made in this book, were strictly economy class, where a man went into the field with a minimum of equipment and at a minimum of comfort. It is very questionable if any of my readers will get a similar chance, as this is something that happens to very few.

Even though I did it, I would not recommend going big game hunting without a professional hunter. These men come high, but they are well worth every cent spent. I can recall many times when a professional hunter would have been most welcome. There is an old saying: "God looks after fools and drunkards." I've wondered, looking back, whether I wasn't in the former category at times.

There are few places in Africa where you could get a big game license without a professional in attendance.

The African safari has something to offer modern man, which can be found in no other place in the world. There is something about a safari that is decidedly different and it affects a man or woman differently than any other experience they could have in this fast moving, hectic world of ours.

Stanley, in his autobiography, had this to say about safaris and it is still true today:

"One of the first sweet and novel pleasures a man can experience in the wilds of Africa is the almost perfect independence; the next, is the almost perfect indifference to all earthly things outside his camp, and that, let people talk as they may, is one of the most exquisite, soul-lulling pleasures a mortal may enjoy."

This chapter was put in the book to offer up-to-date information on safaris and to help you decide which type would suit your budget best. I've called for help on one of the best known and, in my personal opinion, the best safari organization in the United States, the firm of Jonas Brothers of Seattle. They are agents for Uganda and Tanganyika, Ltd.

One of the finest experts on big game hunting in the world today is Bert Klineburger, president of Jonas Brothers. Bert can arrange for de luxe hunting trips to just about any area of the world and will practically guarantee they will be successful. You can rest assured, if you deal with this man, you are getting the personal attention of a man who knows what he is talking about. Just about everything will be planned for you, leaving you to enjoy this unique experience which cannot be matched anywhere else in the world today.

A few years ago, I had the privilege of meeting Bert in his Alaska office at Anchorage. At this time I made application to work for his firm as an apprentice hunter in Uganda. The application got as far as the native office in Kampala, Uganda, and was never heard from again. I'm sure my age was against me.

I have high hopes of making a safari to Africa again in the near future. Sometimes I lay awake at nights thinking about it. It has become almost an obsession with me. This is one of the dangers a man encounters when he has been to this magical country; you want to go back again and again. When I do go, it will be with Jonas Brothers. I'm not sure if it will be a hunting, or a photographic trip. I'd like a better cape buffalo than I have now. There is still room for a sable in my collection, or possibly a situtunga. Bert tells me it will be difficult to better the kudu trophy I already have. Maybe I'll just go and take pictures. I'd be satisfied with that.

Let me give you some prices and information on safaris. In the first place let's consider Mozambique. Later we will discuss in detail, what I consider is the best safari bargain in the world today.

One of the most fertile big game areas in Africa today and one of the most expensive to visit is the Portuguese Province of Mozambique. Safaris into this area are conducted by Nyalaland Safaris, Ltd., of which Jonas Brothers is the North American representative.

This area is remote, but is productive of fine trophies.

Don't get scared off by these preliminary figures, for better news waits for you later on.

These prices are for hunting trips:

	21 days	30 days
One client w/one professional hunter	$3,450	$4,300
Two clients w/one hunter	$5,700	$7,200

Non-hunters going along for the ride and making use of the hunting camp and its facilities are usually charged $30 per day.

In the above charges, the following are not included:

a. Cost of license and extra game coupons.
b. Accommodations in Laurenco Marques.
c. Alcoholic beverages.
d. Custom duties and/or clearance charges.
e. Disinfecting, preparing, crating and shipping trophies.
f. Hire of firearms and ammunition.

Because of redtape involved in the shipping and registration of private firearms, many clients prefer to use company weapons. Costs are as follows:

Heavy caliber rifles, .375 H&H and up	$80 per month
Medium caliber, .270 to .338 H&H	$60 per month
Shotguns	$50 per month

Ammunition is available at local market value.

In addition to the above, a hunter must have in his possession a Model "I" license which costs $107 and is valid for thirty days. It allows him to shoot the following game: one wildebeeste, one zebra, one bushbuck, one crocodile; one hartebeest, one reedbuck, one waterbuck, one impala, two warthogs, two bush pigs, and five small buck.

For other game, the cost of game coupons is below:

Lion	$12.00	Leopard	$14.00
1st elephant	$71.00	Wildebeeste	$ 6.00
2nd elephant	$161.00	Zebra	$15.00
Buffalo	$15.00	Hippo	$20.00
Greater kudu	$15.00	Crocodile	$ 6.00
Sable antelope	$29.00	Warthog	$ 4.00
Nyala	$18.00	Bushpig	$ 4.00
Eland	$29.00	Duiker	$ 2.00
Waterbuck	$ 9.00	Steenbuck	$ 2.00
Hartebeeste	$ 8.00	Chengane	$ 2.00
Reedbuck	$ 8.00	Mangul	$ 2.00
Bushbuck	$ 2.00	Natal duiker	$ 2.00
Impala	$ 4.00		

The safari prices quoted include:

a. Hunting on a private concession.

b. Services of a professional white hunter.

c. Use of the main camp facilities.

d. Use of the mobile camp equipment, including cooks, personal servants, gunbearers, trackers, skinners, drivers and camp assistants.

e. One 4-wheel drive Land Rover for each pro hunter.

f. High quality food. Every effort is made to please individual tastes.

g. A liberal allowance of fine Portuguese table wines if desired and locally manufactured cigarettes of excellent quality.

h. Clearance charges for unaccompanied baggage and transportation of same to camp and return.

i. Transportation by train to and from the hunting area at the beginning and end of trip.

The climate of this area is cool and bracing from April to August and warm clothing should be brought for night use. At this time of the year, there is almost a complete absence of troublesome insects such as flies and mosquitoes, while the tsetse fly does not exist in this area. Some of the finest trophies coming out of Africa today come from this area and it is highly recommended by Mr. Klineburgher. This area borders the Krueger National Park and is a new concession which has only been opened recently.

Maybe you think: "I can't afford that kind of money for a twenty- or thirty-day trip." Then I have good news for you about a new type of safari which has become popular in recent months. This is practically an all-expense safari. Because it is operated under government control, it is much cheaper, without losing any of the deluxe features normally associated with African safaris.

East Africa still offers the finest hunting in the world. It has huge concentrations of game, spectacular natural settings, and a fine climate.

The Uganda and Tanganyika Wildlife Development Companies, which have been formed by the governments of Uganda and Tanzania, bring to you, the dedicated sportsman, fully deluxe, all inclusive safaris, in one or both of these countries. Many of the game sanctuaries which were closed for years are now open for your hunting pleasure and at a price you can now afford.

Let me tell you a little about these countries before I break the good news about prices.

Uganda lies almost in the geographical center of the African continent and is a compact variety of Africa. Here are located the sources of the Nile River, the largest fresh water lake on the continent (Lake Victoria), the fabulous snow-covered Mountains of the Moon (Ruwenzori), and two other large lakes, Edward and Albert. This is the land of the Birunga volcanoes, the home of the mountain gorilla, and the land associated with many of the great names in African exploration. Uganda has great concentrations of game and it is not unusual for a hunter to get as many as ten species of animal from one hunting camp.

Uganda is unusual, too, in that it has regions which can be hunted the year around. From June through November, southern Uganda is at its best. The average elevation of the land is 3,000 to 4,000 feet, which makes for cool nights and days which compare with summer in lower Pennsylvania and New York. Safari itineraries are arranged in accordance with local climatic conditions.

At one time, African safaris took a matter of months. There was a three-week trip by boat. Now with jet transportation, Africa is only 24 hours distant from Kennedy Airport. You are in the hunting area and actually shooting the day after you arrive in Africa. Travel to and from Africa will be on jets of the reliable and efficient Alitalia Airlines which is famous the world over for its gracious Italian warmth and service.

Tanzania is the largest of the three East African countries and contains just about every variety of scenery imaginable.

Most hunting in this vast area will be done in the fantastic Selous Game Sanctuary, or on the Rungwa Game Sanctuary. Both of these areas opened recently, after having been closed for over fifty years. The Selous is so huge, one can drive for days without ever leaving its boundaries. The Rungwa contains some of the finest hunting in Africa, including sable antelope and the illusive greater kudu. June through January is the best time for this area.

This fine new hunting in Africa is due to a new independent government program. The object of the governments of Uganda and Tanzania, in forming their own safari programs, was stated in a newsletter put out by Jonas Brothers of Seattle in May 1965. I quote: . . . "the object, bringing down the price of fully custom deluxe safaris, to encourage more tourists to visit these countries . . . profits would go back into game conservation and game management, where it belongs. The idea was also to educate the natives, that the animals of Africa are a valuable asset to their country, and that each time an animal is shot, a certain fee should go to the local government. There are also large areas which were uninhabited and unhunted, that were bringing in no income . . . it was realized that a crop could be taken from the animals of this area and bring incomes into the countries. For this reason they were opened for hunting. In many instances, the killing of animals helps thin out game herds which have grown too large for the food supply available.

The political situation in all of East Africa remains completely peaceful. Tourists from the United States and Europe are still coming in large numbers. Both governments are going all out for the tourist business. There is a new hotel practically finished in Dar es Salaam, Tanzania, and a large modern hotel has been started in Kampala, Uganda. In the Murchinson Falls National Park, a very beautiful safari lodge is under construction at Chobe, overlooking the Nile. This will accommodate seventy visitors, have a fine restaurant and a swimming pool."

Mr. Klineburgher then went on to say that hunting results during the 1964 season when the Selous Reserve was first opened had been excellent. An airstrip has been completed so that clients can be flown in and many new hunting tracks have been added. Here are some of the trophies taken from this area: several high record book kudus; an elephant with a 141-pound tusk; some outstanding fully maned lion; some record sable; and many other fine trophies.

You may have read the account in June 1965 issue of *True* Magazine, concerning Sam Snead's trip to this area. Several articles on this area have been written by Warren Page of the *Field and Stream* Magazine.

In 1965, the Rungwa Reserve was opened and, due to the abundance of rhino, a limited number are available on both preserves.

Starting in 1966, Tanzania Wildlife will have exclusive hunting rights in all of Tanzania, except for the very western part which will be hunted by Uganda Wildlife.

Here is the information I promised. It will answer questions you may have about the cost to these fabulous areas.

This is the regular deluxe safari, including roundtrip air transportation, New York to New York with 22 days in Africa and 19 days of actual hunting. No license is required on these trips. Rifles and shotguns will be furnished at no extra cost if desired and this will eliminate the cost of shipping and the redtape involved in getting weapon permits for your own guns. Ammunition is available at cost price, per rounds actually used:

Uganda or Tanzania $2,750.00
If you furnish your own transportation to Africa
    and return $1,690.00
One non-hunter may accompany each hunter,
    New York to New York $1,620.00
Non-hunter furnishing transportation ....$ 570.00

Safaris individually tailored to meet clients specifications, inclusive of full deluxe, standard tented accommodations, professional white hunters, hunting cars, use of rifles, etc., can be planned to go anywhere in Uganda, Tanzania, Kenya, or Sudan. Prices quoted are from Kampala, Uganda, or Dar es Salaam, Tanzania. Extra mileage will be charged for safaris going deep into western Tanzania or to Sudan. Charges are for 21 days or over:

One client with professional hunter, per day $120.00
Each additional hunter, per day ....$ 30.00
Each additional non-hunter, per day ....$ 25.00
Each additional white hunter w/hunting car per
  day ....$ 75.00

There is a maximum of two hunters and two non-hunters per each white hunter and hunting car. A maximum of one non-hunter with each hunter, with the exception of photographers. Photographic safaris have a special lower price.

Bongo and situtunga are among the rare trophies which can be hunted on the custom safari. If you want to hunt lion, you must be on a safari of at least 28 days' duration.

On custom safaris, the license is extra and you must pay a trophy fee for each head shot. On the regular safaris, the following game may be shot with no charge for a license unless otherwise noted: buffalo, bushbuck, bush pig, duiker, hartebeeste, dik dik, impala ($15 extra in Uganda), giant forest hog, common reedbuck, chandler's reedbuck ($14 extra in Uganda), southern reedbuck ($14 extra in Tanzania), wart hog, waterbuck ($28 extra in Uganda), oribi ($5 extra in Tanzania), wildebeeste, topi, kob, zebra, sharpe's grysbok, hippo ($28 extra in Uganda), lesser kudu ($28 extra in both countries), eland ($28 extra in both countries), klipspringer ($10 extra in both countries), greater kudu ($56 extra in both countries), leopard ($125 extra in both countries), lion ($140 extra in both countries), sable ($56 extra in both countries), situtunga ($28 extra in both countries). Elephant has a basic charge per animal, plus so much per pound of ivory. In the Selous and Rungwa Areas, an elephant with 200 pounds of ivory would cost $857.30 to shoot.

In both countries, you get the 25-day itinerary, including 19 days of hunting, for $2,650 in Uganda and $2,750 in Tanzania. This includes the round trip air transportation from New York and is less than the cost of a fully equipped compact car. Firearms furnished at no extra cost are:

.30/06, .338 magnum, .375 magnum with scopes
.458 African magnum rifle with open sights
.22 magazine rifles
.12 gauge shotguns
Fishing tackle is also furnished.

Avoid overloading yourself for the trip to Africa. Most of your hunting clothes can be made there within 24 hours and cheaper than you could buy them in the States.

Full medical services are provided on these trips, with anti-malarial drugs and insect repellents furnished. About all you need to bring is your passport, visas, necessary shots, vaccinations, personal effects, and of course your travelers' checks.

How do you live on these safaris? You will have fully purified water to drink, first-class food—served better than in most restaurants—ice, hot showers daily. Your laundry will be done daily and you will sleep in comfort on inner spring mattresses in your own private tent.

One of the major attractions of these safaris is the contrast offered by these comfortable modern camps, found in the middle of the African bush.

Why not be good to yourself and get the thrill of a lifetime while you are still young enough to enjoy it. It will be something you will never forget. Put off buying that new boat, or that second car for another year, and do something you have always dreamed of doing. Take a safari to East Africa. If you would rather take pictures than shoot, this can be arranged too.

You might even wake some morning and find hyenas in your bedroom.

Glossary

AARDVARK—An African mammal which feeds on termites.

ABYSSINIA—The old name for Ethiopia.

ACACIA—A thorny bush or tree found in Africa.

APHRODISIAC—A drug which produces sexual desire.

ATABRINE—A drug used to prevent malaria.

BAG—The quantity of game killed.

BEQ—Bachelor Enlisted Quarters (living quarters for single non-commissioned officers).

BILTONG—Jerked meat.

BLIND—A place of concealment for a hunter.

BOMBA—A fence of thorn bushes erected around a native house or village as protection from wild beasts.

BOSS—The heavy bony structure between the horns of a buffalo.

BUSTARD—A game bird related to the crane.

BWANA—Swahili language for "master" or "boss."

CANINES—The large pointed teeth next to the incisors.

CARNIVOROUS—A meat eating animal.

CARRION—The putrefying flesh of a carcass.

CHEETAH—An Asiatic or African animal of the cat family,

about the size of a leopard, very swift and trained for hunting.

CHINGI—Moslem custom of cutting an animal's throat while it is still alive. Necessary if the meat is to be eaten.

CICADA—An insect of the locust family noted for its shrill, prolonged cry.

COPTIC—The state Church of Ethiopia.

CROSS HAIRS—Referring to the reticule in a telescopic sight.

DUTCH OVEN—A shallow iron kettle used for baking over an open fire.

ENTOURAGE—One's attendants or associates.

ESCARPMENT—A high, steep face of rock such as a long cliff.

FISI—Swahili language for hyena.

FLAGON—A vessel used for liquors, usually with a handle and spout.

FRANCOLINA—Any of a number of partridges found in Africa, having all white meat.

FRANKISH—A member of the confederated German tribes of about the ninth century, hence a native of western Europe.

FROND—A leaf of the palm tree.

GAUGE OR "GA"—Size of the bore of a shotgun.

GOURD—A cleaned, dried vessel made from the gourd vine and used as a drinking vessel.

GUINEA FOWL—A bird with dark, slaty plumage speckled with white which originated in East Africa.

HAKIM—Arabic word for doctor.

HINTERLAND—A region remote from cities and towns.

INDIGENOUS—A native.

ITINERANT—One who travels from one place to another.

KHARTOUM—Capital of Sudan.

LAND ROVER—British-built hunting car similar to a jeep.

LIANA—A tough, clinging vine found in the jungle.

MAIZE—Indian corn.

MASK—The head or face of a wild animal.

MANOUMI—Swahili word for man.

MINARET—The tower of a Moslem mosque.

MORAN—A full-fledged warrior of the Masai tribe.

MOSLEM—A follower of Mohammed; also Mohammedan.

MOSQUE—A Mohammedan temple.

MUEZZIN—A Mohammedan priest.

NIMROD—A hunter.

NOMAD—One of a race or tribe that has no fixed location but wanders from place to place.

OASIS—A green spot in the desert.

OBELISK—A four-sided, usually monolithic pillar, tapering as it rises and terminating in a pyramid.

OUTPOST—A security detachment in front of friendly lines to guard against surprise attack.

OVA—An egg cell.

PAD—The foot of certain animals such as the cat.

PATRIARCH—A venerable old man, usually the head of a family.

PEMMICAN—A preparation of dried meat used by the American Indian.

POACHER—One who takes game illegally.

PREDATOR—An animal that lives by preying on other animals.

PRIMEVAL—Belonging to the first ages.

PROTUBERANCE—A bulge.

PUG—Footprint of a wild animal, usually used when speaking of the cat family.

RAS—An Ethiopian chief.

RONDAVEL—Natives houses found in Kenya and Uganda.

ROGUE—A vicious animal which lives separate from the herd and travels alone.

SAFARI—A hunting expedition.

SARACENS—A nomad of the deserts of Syria and Arabia; a Moslem hostile to the crusaders.

SAURIAN—One of a group of reptiles including the lizard and crocodile.

SCIMITAR—A saber with a curved blade.

SEPSIS—A blood infection caused by bacteria.

SHIFTA—Wandering bandits found in Ethiopia.

SHOAT—A young pig.

SHORED—To strengthen, as with logs.

SIMI—A native knife similar to a machete.

SPOOR—The track of a wild animal.

STYGIAN—Infernal or gloomy.

SUPER-POSED—A gun, usually smoothbore with barrels one on top of the other.

TEMBA—Swahili word for "elephant".

TOTO—Swahili word for "little" or "baby".

TRACKER—A native skilled in following the tracks of wild animals.

TSETSE FLY—An African fly which carries the parasite causing human sleeping sickness.

TYRO—A beginner.

VELDT—Grassland of Africa in which are scattered shrubs and trees.

WATER HOLE—A spot in the veldt either natural or man made, where water is found.

WEBLEY—Revolvers used by the British armed forces.

WHETTING—To sharpen a knife.

WITHERS—The ridge between the shoulder bones of an animal.

WOG—British term, usually sarcastic for "Westernized Oriental Gentleman."